Concern for the Church
in the World

CONCERN for the Church in the World

Essays on Christian Responsibility,
1958–1963

CONCERN: A Pamphlet Series for
Questions of Christian Renewal

EDITED BY
Laura Schmidt Roberts

WIPF & STOCK · Eugene, Oregon

CONCERN FOR THE CHURCH IN THE WORLD
Essays on Christian Responsibility, 1958–1963

CONCERN: A Pamphlet Series for Questions of Christian Renewal

Copyright © 2022 Wipf and Stock Publishers. All rights reserved. Except for brief quotations in critical publications or reviews, no part of this book may be reproduced in any manner without prior written permission from the publisher. Write: Permissions, Wipf and Stock Publishers, 199 W. 8th Ave., Suite 3, Eugene, OR 97401.

Wipf & Stock
An Imprint of Wipf and Stock Publishers
199 W. 8th Ave., Suite 3
Eugene, OR 97401

www.wipfandstock.com

PAPERBACK ISBN: 978-1-7252-6092-4
HARDCOVER ISBN: 978-1-7252-6093-1
EBOOK ISBN: 978-1-7252-6094-8

03/08/22

Contents

Series Foreword | vii
Introduction by Laura Schmidt Roberts | xi

Part I: On Christian Responsibility in and for the "World"

1 Nonresistance and Responsibility | 3
  GORDON D. KAUFMAN

2 A Second Look at Responsibility | 24
  ALBERT J. MEYER

3 Nonresistance and Responsibility: A Critical Analysis | 32
  DAVID HABEGGER

4 The Otherness of the Church | 39
  JOHN HOWARD YODER

Part II: On Political Ideologies: Articles from *Concern* 10 (1961)

5 Christian Thought in the Age of the Cold War | 53
  JAN M. LOCHMANN

6 Christians and Marxists | 63
  ALBERT GAILLARD

7 Where Are the Firemen? | 72
  KATHARINA VAN DRIMMELEN

CONTENTS

8 The Christian Answer to Communism | 79
   JOHN HOWARD YODER

9 Marginalia | 86
   JOHN HOWARD YODER

Part III: On Kingdom Economics (*CONCERN* 11, 1963)

10 Poverty | 99
    KARL BARTH

11 The Poverty of Christ | 103
    ANDREW MURRAY

12 Money | 111
    R. MEHL

13 God or Mammon | 119
    VIRGIL VOGT

14 Marginalia | 163
    JOHN HOWARD YODER

Contemporary Response

15 All Economy Is Atheist: Towards a Non-competitive Hope for the Church in the World | 167
    MELISSA FLORER-BIXLER

Appendix: Listing of all *CONCERN* republication volumes | 175
Bibliography | 183

Series Foreword to the 2022 Edition

In 1952 a group of seven young American Mennonite intellectuals studying in Europe convened for a two-week theological retreat in Amsterdam to discuss the place of Mennonites in what they saw as the modern, "post-Christendom" world. Most all had come to post-war Europe with Canadian or American Mennonite organizations to assist mission, relief, and rebuilding efforts. They are, in the words of one participant, overwhelmed by what they encounter—the theology, imagery, procedures, and practices they bring are inadequate to their work and witness in postwar Europe. They have many questions about what it means to be the church—to be disciples—in that time and place; questions compounded by conversations and studies that open up for them the ideological and philosophical currents sweeping Europe at the time.

What becomes clear in the papers presented in Amsterdam and the subsequently published series *Concern: A Pamphlet Series for Questions of Christian Renewal* (1954–71) is a common concern over a gap between an Anabaptist vision and contemporary Mennonite reality.[1] They view the increasingly hierarchical denominational structure of the Mennonite church in Canada and the United States and its institution-building as inconsistent with an Anabaptist notion of church as community. These structural forms and the accompanying concerns for their perpetuation reflect "Protestantizing" compromise instead of Anabaptist movement-oriented, mission-minded, evangelical zeal. The writers instead call for a more radical and authentic expression of the Christian life. They call for a renewal that would

---

1. Toews, *Mennonites in American Society*, 232. For more on the historical genesis of *Concern* see the front pieces of Vogt, *Roots of CONCERN*, and Hershberger, "Power, Tradition, and Renewal."

realign the mission, leadership, and organization of the church as well as its relationship to broader society in ways more resonant with the tenets of a culturally-engaged Anabaptism; which is to say, they call for a Mennonite response to modernity which is both faithful to their construal of Anabaptist tradition and appropriate to the times.[2]

While *Concern: A Pamphlet Series for Questions of Christian Renewal* and the movement it inspired address the context of the day, the call issued to discern what it means to be a faithful church in and for the times—ever the church's call—is one we face with growing urgency in today's postmodern context. What theology, imagery, and practices are adequate to the work and witness of disciples in this time and place? What is church *for*? Republishing these essays makes more readily available for this task resources shaped by Anabaptist tradition. The themes and issues the essays raise remain relevant: Christian responsibility in and to the "world," the goal of history, critical engagement with political ideologies and economic theories, global mission and the colonial legacy of Christendom, the unavoidably enculturated nature of lived faith, the gifts of the Spirit, desire for renewed (radicalized?) authentic expressions of faith, Anabaptist-shaped church structure and pastoral leadership, the fraught realities of communal authority and discipline.

But the model the pamphlet series provides is equally important. Especially at its inception, *Concern* was intended to be a forum for works in progress versus polished churchly or academic pieces—a place to test ideas, raise questions, challenge practices, even change one's mind. The pamphlets present articles reflecting varying viewpoints intended to promote discussion, critical reflection, and ultimately transformation of understanding, practices, and structured forms of Christian discipleship. This example of dialog across difference as a shared path toward renewal is welcome in the current increasingly polarized context, where disagreement seems more likely to end a conversation than begin one.

Response essays from contemporary Mennonite writers in each volume continue in this vein, critically engaging the contribution and limitations of the historical essays and building out concerns of their own in the current global, ecclesial, and historical climate. One aspect of that climate is especially important to state clearly: the mixed legacy of *Concern* writer

---

2. See Vogt, "Foreword," in *The Roots of CONCERN*. Sawatsky, "Editorial," iii. *The Conrad Grebel Review* 8.2 contains articles on and reflections by participants in the *Concern* movement.

and sometime editor, theologian and ethicist John Howard Yoder, whose sexual abuse must be acknowledged.³ The depth and breadth of harm Yoder perpetrated, most horrifically on those he abused, and also on the shape and substance of Anabaptist-Mennonite theology and ecclesiology, is difficult to fathom. While significant deconstruction of Yoder's work has been done, grappling with the aftermath and implications continues.⁴ Refusing to engage or promote Yoder's work as a whole or selectively is one avenue of response. Such selectivity is evident in this series; most, but not all, of Yoder's essays have been republished here. Some material already widely available, and especially the content or use of which harmed victim-survivors of Yoder's abuse, has not been included. Another avenue of response takes encounters with his thought (in church, in institutions, in print) as an occasion to reframe discussion of it: by first speaking the truth of his serial sexual abuse and then reconsidering his work in light of that context. This series also does some of that work selectively, at the choice of several contemporary response writers and in this acknowledgment prefacing each volume. *Concern* should not be reduced to Yoder's contributions. While persistent, Yoder's voice is but one among many across the original pamphlets. On their own, the other fifty-plus writers give rich, contextualized, and diverse expression to theological, ecclesiological, and missiological explorations in the mid-twentieth century.

A historical republication project such as this is not possible without the expert help of librarians and archivists. I owe such debts in too many places to name but the greatest—to Fresno Pacific University's Hiebert Library Director Kevin Enns-Rempel, archivist Hannah Keeney, and research librarian David Hasegawa—must be mentioned. I have benefitted from the university's support through a sabbatical leave dedicated to this project, multiple Provost's Faculty Research Grants, and the Fresno Pacific Biblical Seminary's Center for Anabaptist Studies donation toward publication costs. I greatly appreciate other contributions toward those costs from the Schafer-Friesen Research Fund (Goshen College), the Gerhard Lohrenz

---

3. See Waltner Goossen, "'Defanging the Beast.'" Waltner Goossen catalogs both Yoder's serial sexual abuse and institutional failure to respond adequately to his victims or Yoder himself.

4. In addition to the many articles in *Mennonite Quarterly Review* 89.1, see for example Anabaptist Mennonite Biblical Seminary, "AMBS Response to Victims"; Cramer et al., "Theology and Misconduct"; "On Teaching John Howard Yoder" collection of essays by Mennonite faculty from various institutions in *Mennonite Life* 68 (2014); Soto Albrecht and Stephens, eds. *Liberating the Politics of Jesus.*

Publication Fund (Canadian Mennonite University), and the Conrad Grebel University College Theological Studies Program. I am especially grateful to the Mennonite Faith and Learning Society (British Columbia), whose work first became known to me through its sponsorship of the Humanitas Anabaptist Centre (Trinity Western University), and whose very generous support of this publication shows concretely their stated commitment to advance education and scholarship from an Anabaptist perspective.

Thanks are due to Fresno Pacific colleagues in the Division of Biblical and Religious Studies, especially Quentin Kinnison, to Rod Janzen, and to Larry Dunn, for unflagging support, probing questions, and insightful feedback along the way. This project would not have come to me without Ched Myers' suggestion and encouragement, and would not have come to completion without the steadfast guidance and input of Ted Lewis at Wipf and Stock. Thank you both for the gift of this work. Finally, I am deeply grateful to the contemporary response writers in each volume of the series whose essays model so well what Paul Ricoeur would call a "refiguring" of tradition. Thank you for grappling with the plurality and ambiguity of tradition in ways that challenge and potentially revitalize it through theology and praxis from and for actual current ecclesial communities, Anabaptist and otherwise.

An appendix in each book in this series lists the contents of the seven total volumes comprising the *Concern* republication project initiated under the editorial direction of Virgil Vogt which this series completes.[5]

Laura Schmidt Roberts

Fresno Pacific University
September 2021

---

[5]. In addition to this four-volume, thematically organized series, three other volumes complete the Wipf and Stock republication of the *Concern* pamphlets: Vogt, *Roots of CONCERN* and *CONCERN for Education*; Vogt and Roberts, *Concern for Anabaptist Renewal*.

Introduction

While the *Concern* pamphlet series initially focused on issues of Anabaptist-Mennonite renewal, these essays demonstrate the broadening of scope and contributors that occurred.¹ Editorial comments ("Marginalia") from original *Concern* 5–7 (1958–59) underscore *Concern* as a vehicle of conversation across denominational, academic, theological, and ideological lines. "Dissenting" contributions, including those seriously challenging customary ways of expressing aspects of Christian faith, are solicited and published in dialog. Articles republished here and the discussion surrounding them demonstrate *Concern*'s specific interest in creating space for views in tension with those acceptable to the Mennonite hierarchy (and to some extent a broader Mennonite majority) at the time. Thus the volume begins with several pieces exploring real tensions between a commitment to nonviolence and questions of social responsibility—a debate that documents the way views on the long-standing Mennonite commitment to pacifism were in flux mid twentieth-century.

By then turning to essays addressing political ideologies and economics, this volume makes concrete the wider range of application raised by the initial discussion of a pacifist-informed Christian responsibility in and for the world. Editorial comments from *Concern* 10 (1961) identify a pervasive and growing Marxism as the shared context tying together the pamphlet's essays, observing the struggle of US Christians of the day to respond. Marxism's mixed nature ("neither all right nor all wrong") and its comprehensiveness as an ideology call for a thoughtful, enacted response. Similarly, the content of *Concern* 11 (1963) circles around another shared

---

1. For the origins and context of *Concern: A Pamphlet Series for Questions of Christian Renewal* (1954–71) please see the Series Foreword to this volume.

contextual concern: the challenge the affluence of Western society presents to Christian faithfulness. Editorial comments in that volume explain that the pamphlet's focus on economics arises from numerous conversations among the *Concern* organizers and from their conviction that Jesus's teaching on "the unseating of Mammon" should be taken seriously. These essays are an important part of the mid twentieth-century North American Mennonite story; they model engagement with contextual challenges across intentionally diverse perspectives, and in so doing raise issues that remain relevant to this day.

In the first section, "On Christian Responsibility in and for the 'World,'" Gordon Kaufman's essay (1958) opens debate over the nature of a Christian pacifist ethic, the nature of the church-world dichotomy informing such an ethic, and the nature of the love to which Christ calls his followers as central to that ethic. For Kaufmann the Christian responsibility to love means a humble posture of unqualified self-giving in support of the other. For Albert Meyer (1958) the responsibility of love has more "content" in reflecting a primary allegiance to Christ and the way of Christ. David Habegger (1959) asserts the righteousness and justice of Christian love (the "ought" of God in contrast to the "is" of society), but insists Christian responsibility is not to love but to redeem/ bring others to Christ. John Howard Yoder[2] (1960) presents a theological framework for renegotiating these church-"world" and church-state relationships in a context he describes as the end of the Constantinian era,[3] emphasizing the church's unique role and a particular understanding of history and its goal.

The remainder of the volume turns from the above broader discussion to concrete examples engaging issues of church, "world," Christian

---

2. This volume contains work by John Howard Yoder, whose sexual abuse is a well-established fact which must be acknowledged. Please see the Foreword for more about the editor's choice to republish Yoder's work in this series.

3. While widely used today, references to the end of Constantinianism/Christendom, post-Constantinianism, and post-Christendom are contested for the ways in which such terms can mask how, as Ron Adams and Isaac Villegas put it, Christians still "benefit from the institutional prominence of cultural Christianity as it shapes our society." The authors explain that "Christendom names a social arrangement in which Christianity penetrates the structures of power. . . . Our argument is that such an era has not ended, that the era of politically powerful Christian institutions is not dying, that we do not live in a 'post' Christendom age. Instead, Christendom is reinventing itself as it mutates into a new form: call it neo-Christendom. This mutation differs from the political system of the Medieval Ages yet retains the same preference for Christian sociopolitical ascendency." See Adams and Vallegas, "Post-Christendom or Neo-Christendom?"

responsibility, and the goal of history. The second section, "On Political Ideologies," does so in relationship to the Cold War and Marxist/communist ideologies, presenting the contents of the original *Concern* 10 (1961). The third section—the original *Concern* 11 (1963)—explores concrete questions of poverty, wealth, and economics in relationship to kingdom allegiance and its accompanying economy.

The response essay by Melissa Florer-Bixler pursues this intersection of peace theology, economics, and political ideology by contrasting the historical essays with the work and words of Dorothy Day from the same time period. Florer-Bixler questions the *Concern* writers' uncritical acceptance of democracy wedded to capitalism which accompanies their wariness of Marxism and communism. Recounting Day's reflections on the disparity between the Catholic Church as an institution that thrives under capitalism and Jesus's call of mission to the poor, Florer-Bixler poses this question: "If the church will survive as a minority kingdom among the corrupted Rom 13 power of the state apparatus, why decide for free market capitalism disguised as democracy, especially as the United States watches black and Latino workers struggle under this system? Why put our trust here, as if in this we were free from capitulation to an economic system?" She calls for honest reflection today that interrogates our participation in economic systems so that in this arena of life also we may make manifest the good news for all people.

Florer-Bixler's call for a more robust and self-critical theology of economics implies the need for a theologically-derived politics—a political theology—suitable to the challenges of the day, both for the writers of *Concern* and for our time. This volume has presented the historical exploration of those concerns as making concrete the wider range of application raised by the mid twentieth-century discussion of a pacifist-informed Christian responsibility in and for the world. In our time, what peace theology is adequate for such tasks? Contemporary Mennonite theologian and ethicist, Malinda E. Berry argues the language of nonviolence in the tradition of Dr. Martin Luther King Jr. (vs. pacifism) more suitably grounds such a theology, for it more clearly and broadly proclaims a gospel that renounces all violence. She explains:

> Looking back, we can see that if we reduce peace theology to avoiding conflict, then it will only ever be a theo-ethics of privilege. And if we reduce it to an orientation of personal obedience to communal norms, then it will only ever be a peculiar form of

discipleship. If, however, we enact a peace theology as a theo-ethics seeking shalom as a way of imagining God's politics, then our witness becomes a form of social engagement with the world that hopes for personal and communal transformation. Shalom is a way of invoking the power of life's goodness despite the suffering, exploitation, violence, and alienation that remind us that evil is as powerful as ever. Shalom is invested in the quality of our living and loving. Shalom paints vivid pictures of opposites embracing—unlikely allies laughing with abandon as they break bread together, wolves and lambs enjoying the shade of the same tree, an unshakeable sense that we belong.[4]

What does it mean to welcome God's shalom into our lives and our world? Berry constructs a Shalom Political Theology, a multidimensional shalom marked by practices of transparent naming of influential members of communities, nonviolent communication, and circle process. These practices integrate her construals of nonviolence ("the politics of shalom"), non-conformity, and what it means to be human more broadly. Peace theology framed as nonviolence instead of pacifism underscores human agency and the fragility of human freedom "in a society with the power to structure our lives in ways that distort our dignity and confine our choices." This context—our context—for Berry necessitates clearer, full-orbed renouncement of violence. Such a call articulates a vision of renewal for our time, one that resonates with and moves beyond the concerns of the historical essays, exploring "a new type of Mennonite peace theology for a new era of discipleship."[5]

---

4. Berry, "Shalom Political Theology," 73.

5. Anabaptist-Mennonite political theology has received renewed attention recently. See for example *Political Theology* 22.3; *The Conrad Grebel Review* 37.1 and 36.3; Reimer, *Toward an Anabaptist*. Reimer's sketch, published posthumously, distinguishes between a theologically-derived politics and politically-derived theology.

Part I

On Christian Responsibility in and for the "World"

1

Nonresistance and Responsibility

Gordon D. Kaufman

I

Modern Christian pacifists and nonpacifists seem to hold in common at least one assumption about Christian ethics: that an ethic founded in nonresistant love leads inevitably to withdrawal from and failure to take responsibility for the social order, and, conversely, that an ethic which concerns itself with the exigencies of the social order must in some way compromise or even give up nonresistant love as its sole ethical norm and imperative. Beginning from this assumption, the "Christian realism" of a man like Reinhold Niebuhr insists that love is an "impossible possibility" for a man as a participant in the realities of social life, and that the best that can be hoped for in this age is some approximation to "justice" gained through and supported by the power of the state. The Christian as well as the non-Christian ought to help achieve and maintain such justice, even though to do so requires, as Niebuhr is convinced, that he forsake the Christian ideal of absolute nonresistance.[1] Starting from the same assumption, contemporary advocates of the historic Mennonite strategy of withdrawal from the responsibilities of the sociopolitical order insist anew that the serious Christian disciple, whose basic motivation and objective

---

1. Niebuhr's position is set forth in various places. See especially *An Interpretation of Christian Ethics* and "Why the Christian Church Is Not Pacifist." His most recent statement on the subject appears in an article written in collaboration with Dun, "God Wills Both Justice and Peace."

is nonresistant love, cannot participate in the power struggles of a non-Christian world.[2] A tacit admission of the same dichotomy is present in the widespread liberal-pacifist interpretation of the political relevance of Christian ethics in terms of the watered-down notion of "nonviolent resistance" instead of the more radical and difficult notion of nonresistance. Though each of these positions differs sharply from the others, they all agree on the disparity, and even the contradiction, between the realities and necessities of the social order and radical nonresistance.

Acceptance of this dichotomy leaves theological ethics, as well as the acting Christian, in a very difficult position, for it implies that the basic orientation of Christian ethics removes it from concern with the deepest problems of society. One then must bypass the specifically Christian ethical consciousness, either through invoking Old Testament ethics (after the manner of Calvin) or "orders of creation" (after the manner of Brunner) or "natural law" (after the manner of the Thomists) as somehow level with or even taking precedence over the ethics of Jesus; or through showing that the radicalness of Jesus's ethic was a function of and essentially relevant only to his own eschatological expectations of the imminent end of the world (Schweitzer) and that therefore Jesus could ignore a problem which is nevertheless fundamental to our situation; or through insisting on the radical otherness of God's demands from man's—even redeemed man's—possibilities, an otherness so great that it is necessary to invoke principles and criteria for decision-making which have no clearly Christian basis (Reinhold Niebuhr). Each of these positions involves the attempt to find some locus outside of the specifically Christian consciousness of the demand for nonresistant love, which locus can then serve as the basis for developing an ethic of society and can serve as a guide to the Christian in his life in the world. Needless to say, all such positions suffer the theological embarrassment of not being based clearly in the Christian revelation. It would seem, then, that one whose ethic is based on the revelation in Jesus Christ is forced by the apparent dichotomy between love and the social order to withdraw from the power struggles.

But such withdrawal proves to be theologically quite as embarrassing as attempted participation, for it leads to the negation of the very love in the name of which the withdrawal is made. If the nature of Christian love be understood in terms of the teaching of the Sermon on the Mount, on

---

2. See especially John Howard Yoder's articles "Reinhold Niebuhr and Christian Pacifism" and "The Anabaptist Dissent."

the one hand, and God's action of condescension, self-giving, and sacrifice unto death (Phil 2: 1–11), on the other, then love must always be understood as just that which never retreats from an evil situation, but always advances into it totally without regard for itself. The more evil is the situation, the more urgent is the demand on love to become involved redemptively. We Mennonites have interpreted the injunction to love our enemies far too simply and too negatively as meaning that we should avoid getting into fights with those who do not agree with us. But this quietist interpretation is more stoic than Christian. Love is not that which keeps out of trouble, a means of remaining above and secure from the conflicts of this world. Love is precisely that which goes into the very heart of an evil situation and attempts to rectify it. Relief programs in which we attempt to minister to the needs of the world in the midst of the evils of war and hate are not enough. However concerned we are and ought to be about physical and spiritual suffering, as Christians we know that the real evil in human affairs is not suffering but sin. It is in the midst of sinful situations that love must be found working, if it is love at all, and the more sinful the situation, the greater is the imperative that love enter it. Every pagan form of goodness attempts to avoid sin at all costs; Christian love on the contrary expresses itself precisely in its drive into the very heart of sin. The Christian, if there is a Christian, must be one who is the very friend of sinners (Matt 11:19; Luke 7:34).

Love, then, in sharp contrast with every other conception of goodness, is that which is concerned precisely to relate itself to its enemies, to sinners. Love is in fact not a "that" at all which can exist in and by itself; love exists only as a relationship, a relationship in which one person gives or sacrifices everything in himself, not for those who deserve such sacrifice nor for those who love him, but just for those who would destroy him. God's love for man is evident not in that God loved man because man loved God, but in that while man was in enmity and rebellion against God, God was actively reconciling man to himself (Rom 5:10; 1 John 4:10, 19). The Christian is not simply called on to love those who love him and are members of the "beloved community"; even the publicans and the gentiles do that (Matt 5:46, 47). Insofar as the love, i.e., the dynamic self sacrificial self-giving of the Christian disciple and the Christian community, is directed largely to members of that community, the community is little different from the communities of paganism. The life of the Christian disciple and the Christian community must consist in the constant attempt to give unselfishly to just those persons and communities and forces which seem most bent on destroying it. Christian love, as perfectly exemplified in God's act in Christ, sacrifices itself for and to sin; Christian love gives itself to its own enemies. This self-sacrifice and self-giving to the evils of the sinful situation is so radical and thorough and complete that Saint Paul finds it necessary to say that in its perfect expression, Christ, "who knew no sin" was made "to be sin . . . so that in him we might become the righteousness of God" (2 Cor 5:21).

Love goes to the very heart of the most sinful situations that it can find, and there it gives of itself without any reservation whatsoever. This is the absurdity of the Christian ethic; it is an ethic of radical imprudence. The Anabaptist-Mennonite tradition has always tried to interpret love in the radical sense of the New Testament, but in its tendency to withdraw from participation in the power struggles of the world it has badly compromised itself. On the Mennonite view, it is just in the power struggles, where self-centered and selfish individuals and groups attempt to dominate others and subject them, that are to be found both the essence and the most terrible expression of sin. For this reason, Mennonites have felt unable to participate in these struggles. And yet, it is the character of love, not that it retreats from its opposite, but that it rushes in trying to act redemptively. Though certainly one cannot attempt to dominate others in the name of love, neither can one ever withdraw from sinful situations of attempted domination in the name of love. The tendency in the Anabaptist-Mennonite tradition has been to see clearly the first side of this paradox and to neglect the other side. And from this has followed the conviction that we have a right—nay, even a duty—to withdraw from certain aspects of human life and society simply because we think those aspects are sinful. But this is failing to love, just as certainly as is action out of the sinful desire to dominate. In sharp opposition to any strategy of withdrawal, which is always motivated by the kind of love known to the publicans and gentiles, Christian love always takes responsibility for the sinful situation.[3]

3. It should be evident from this discussion that the notion of "Responsibility" as a category of Christian ethics is neither simply an axiom which is taken for granted but has no theological basis, nor does it find its theological justification in terms of a doctrine of sin. Yoder seems to think these are the roots of the notion of responsibility (see "Anabaptist Dissent," esp. 57–68) though elsewhere ("Reinhold Niebuhr and Christian Pacifism," 113), while also arguing this view, he admits that "there exists a real Christian responsibility for the social order, but that responsibility is a derivative of Christian love." This is essentially the position I am maintaining, and some implications of which I am trying to develop.

The crucial question, then, is not whether as Christians we have some sort of responsibility for the social and political orders in which we live, but rather, what is the nature of that responsibility, and how must it express itself? It should be clear at the outset that this responsibility that we have for the society in which we live is not simply an outgrowth of or rationalization of the fact that we happen to belong to a certain group and a certain nation. Certainly we have obligations to these groups deriving from the fact that God has created us in and through a people who have given of themselves for us; and our response to his (and their) gifts to us should be one of gratitude and awareness of special obligations owed both to the Creator and to those through whom he brought us into being: the family, the community, the nation, etc. But our responsibility for the social order goes beyond the necessity to respond to the fact and nature of our creation. As Christians, our responsibility derives more directly and more decisively from God's action as Redeemer, from God's action in Jesus Christ. It is the obligation laid on us to love our brother as our proper response to God's prior love for us that is the basis for our concern for the social context in which our brother lives. Our responsibility for our brother in all aspects of his being derives from the necessity of our being responsive to God's love and mercy towards us. Conversely, it is not possible to respond to God's love or be obedient to his demand without taking responsibility for our brother. Responsibility for the brother and responsibility for the society of which he (as well as we) is a part thus derives directly from our responsibility to God. It is a religious responsibility from which no evasion of any kind is possible, and it must be taken with absolute seriousness.

II

The responsibility laid upon us for our fellow men may be conveniently analyzed in terms of three aspects. The first is accepted in some form in all lines of the Christian tradition, and hence need not be developed in detail here. It may be described as our evangelistic or missionary responsibility: our responsibility to preach the gospel. God has given us the opportunity and laid upon us the obligation to witness to the truth of his revelation in Jesus Christ, to make him known to all men. Sometimes this task of witnessing has been interpreted in the narrow terms of simply speaking certain words or distributing tracts or something of the sort, but the Mennonite tradition has always known that this witness must be in the deepest sense a witness of the whole life. Our words no doubt must point to what God has done, but unless our lives have been transformed and themselves give witness to God's love, our words are empty. God's redemption is not merely an intellectual thing, but something that involves the totality of man's existence and being, and therefore it is with the totality of his being that man must speak of God's grace. The first aspect of our responsibility to our fellow men is, then, so to live and speak that we witness to God's love for man. We must preach, we must freely and willingly do deeds of service and mercy, we must participate in a community in which the members truly love one another.

But simply witnessing to the truth as we see the truth does not exhaust the responsibilities of the Christian disciple toward his fellows. Witnessing is an expression of our love for our fellow, but love is more than simply witnessing. It is, in fact, possible to witness without love, as did Jonah, and as does anyone who points the finger of scorn and judgment on his neighbor or his society but does not so sympathize with the sufferings of that society as to participate in them himself. If the action of God in Christ is our model of love, it becomes clear that love is not something that stands afar off, as it were, and shouts a "witness" to those for whom it takes responsibility. This is in fact precisely the difference between the Old Testament and the New. In the former, God sent his word via his messengers, the prophets and others; in the latter, he himself came into human society to share in the grief and sin of human existence. Witnessing, taken by itself, can very easily become an attempt to do precisely the reverse of love, namely to manipulate others, to bring others to a change in belief and life in accordance with what we happen to think is right. The fanatic, the persecutor, the inquisitor of every age, are all witnesses to their faith, and in many cases, they think it is Christian faith to which they are witnessing. Love does more than simply witness to its own convictions: love has real concern for the other as he actually is, not simply as I happen to think that he ought to be. As Brunner has put it: "To love a human being means to accept his existence, as it is given to me by God, and thus to love him as he is. For only if I love him thus, that is, as this particular sinful person, do I love him. For this is what he really is. Otherwise I love an idea—and in the last resort this means that I am merely loving myself."[4]

This has important consequences for our problem of the expression of our responsibility to our neighbor. For this means that the first and

---

4. Brunner, *Divine Imperative*, 129.

primary thing that is required of me, if I am to act in love, is not that I try to impose myself or my ideas on the other as though I were God with absolute truth in my hand, but that I accept the other as a person, as one who has his own integrity in his own right. Above all else I must not violate or lead him to violate his own convictions and the integrity of his own personal existence which he—as I myself—has from and before God. We cannot excuse ourselves from this second aspect of love through saying that it is only the person of the fellow Christian whom we must treat with such respect, that the person of the sinner who is outside the fold is to be preached to with no such concerns. For this is to violate the nature of love as it is revealed to us in the New Testament. God does not honor the freedom and integrity only of believers, acting as a dictatorial tyrant toward sinners. God does not force sinners to turn toward him against their will. It is just the sinner whom God loves so much that he actually sacrifices himself so that the sinner, in his own freedom and out of the gratitude welling up within him, may turn to God. If God's *agape* is the model of the love expected of the Christian, then we must always act toward even the worst sinner with the utmost respect for him as a personal being, one who is himself responsible to God.

This means that in our attempt to love our neighbor, there must not be, in the first place, condemnation of the other for his ideas or his actions or his very being, but rather acceptance of the other as a fellow creature of God for whom Christ also died, acceptance of him as a brother. Our brotherly concern for him will not lead us to begin immediately with condemning him for his sins; rather, it will lead us to try sympathetically to understand his situation as he himself understands it and thus to try to appreciate his own efforts to see the truth and the right and to live by them, however much these efforts may differ or even contradict our own position. As Christians we will not insist on his living in the precise relation to God which happens to be our own, for this would be trying to play the role of the Mediator ourselves, trying to be the Christ. We will rather be concerned that his own unique and independent relation to God through Christ be deepened. As Christians, our love will not express itself through the attempt to make our brother over in our own image—this is the epitome of sin. It will express itself rather in our acceptance of him as he is, whoever he is—and even our making ourselves as much like him as we can—in the hope that thus may we be the instrument through which God may transform him into his will—something possibly quite different from our conception of his will for our brother. "For though I am free from all men, I have made myself a slave to all, that I might win the more. To the Jews I became as a Jew, in order to win Jews; to those under the law I became as one under the law—though not being myself under the law—that I might win those under the law. To those outside the law I became as one out-side the law—not being without law toward God but under the law of Christ—that I might win those outside the law. To the weak I became weak, that I might win the weak. I have become all things to all men, that I might by all means save some" (1 Cor 9:19–22).

The second aspect, then—though first in order of importance—of our love for our neighbor is the acceptance of him as a person, giving full honor to his insights into the truth and the right and his duty trying to help him deepen his own relationship with God in Christ, rather than simply making him into our own disciple. For those of us who are heir to the Anabaptist-Mennonite tradition, with its insistence on the theological necessity for religious liberty, this should be a self-evident point. It has, nevertheless, some hard consequences for us. In regard to the problem of nonresistance specifically, it implies that we have no right—if we are truly disciples of Christ acting out of love—to preach from the housetops that we have the true faith and the true understanding of the Christian life, all others to the contrary notwithstanding. It means just the opposite. It means that we must express our love to our neighbor, whether he claims to be Christian or not, through first listening to his understanding of what is demanded of him by God. It means that we must be more concerned to help him to see clearly the implications of his own insights into God's commands than to denounce him for not interpreting God's commands as we interpret them. It means our first concern must be for his integrity as a responsible agent before God, not for our interpretation of the gospel. For freedom and spontaneity and openness in his relationship to God, Christ has set him free; let us be careful, therefore, that we do not attempt to impose upon him a new yoke of slavery to our ideas of what that relationship to God should entail (Gal 5:1).

Most Christian pacifists, I suppose, would accept in substance what has been said here, at least as it applies to cases of individual counseling in which they become involved. Thus if a young man, troubled about whether he should go into the army or become a conscientious objector, asks help, most pacifists would do all they could to help him come to a clearer and deeper understanding of what his own convictions already are and what the implications of those convictions might be for his present decision. Beyond this, most pacifists would no doubt try to explain their own understanding of the implications of the Christian faith on the issue of war, and would try to help him see why they think a pacifist position is required of a Christian. But surely no one has the right to say to the other: this is what you must decide, this is God's will for you. The decision as to what he must do is something which each must make for himself in his own confrontation with the God who made himself known in Jesus Christ. No one else has the right to play the role of the Mediator and to tell him what God requires of him. Nor does anyone else have the right to relieve him of the responsibility of making his own decision himself and bearing the consequences thereof. To do so is to attempt to dominate the other—the very reversal of love—and to try to frustrate his attempt to be the responsible and free person which God has created him to be. To do so is to demand that a man decide and live by a faith which is not his own, and the consequences of which, therefore, he will not be prepared to bear, ending, as they have in the past and may again in the future, in the cross. To do so is to forget that "Christian discipleship is a matter of individual calling and response," and therefore we should "not expect Christian ethics of the non-Christian."[5]

This has important implications, also, for our attitude toward society, and our expectations of society. Societies, as individuals, are guided in their actions by moral insights and appreciation of moral values, and hence, in a certain sense, societies also must be treated as free and responsible moral agents. Thus, the sensitivity to moral values in American society is such that enslavement of other humans is no longer acceptable to that society as a whole (though it might well be to many individuals in the society), and this sensitivity has become incorporated in the laws and customs and mores of the society. On the other hand, the sensitivity of our society to economic inequalities and injustices and to the horrors of atomic warfare is not as highly developed as in some other contemporary nations. The actions of our nation, as of all nations, result not only from the power factors that play around it, but also from the context of moral values and insights carried and kept alive in the mores, customs and laws of the country, a context which provides norms in terms of which the nation "decides" what it "ought to do" in the circumstances confronting it. This context is of course never precisely definable, nor is it the same in all parts of the community. The mores of the deep South are somewhat different from the North on the

5. Yoder, "Anabaptist Dissent," 46.

matter of relations between the races, and the mores of one small homogeneous community, e.g., the Hutterites, may be quite at variance from those of the surrounding peoples. But despite all variations and ambiguities, the context is always there as a factor whenever a community or society acts as a social unit. Societies, just as individuals, may be sensitive to and responsive to moral insights and values and even to the demands of God laid upon them, and because of this capacity, societies also may be sinful. Not only the Christian church, but every social group, must be understood as such a morally and religiously responsible agent.[6]

Our attitude, therefore, as Christians toward the actions and beliefs of a society, whether our own or some other, must be analogous to our attitude toward a fellow man who has come to us for counsel. Before preaching fiery denunciations of the evil and sin which we see before us, we must lovingly and sympathetically attempt to accept what is before us in all its sinfulness. We must attempt to understand what are the insights and the values which govern the society and try to see what it means to live believing them to come from God himself. We must, in other words, be just as sympathetic and understanding, and just as unwilling to impose our own will, on the society of which we are a part, as we would be in the case of an individual whom we truly love. Our desire here, as there, must be to help the society come to a deeper understanding of its own deepest convictions before God, and help it to see more clearly the implications of the various courses of action which lie before it. For example, we must not, as too often pacifists have, simply witness against every military bill that comes before Congress. This is indeed part of our obligation, our obligation to witness. But we who know well that it is folly to expect non-Christians to act as Christians and to expect Christians whose understanding of the faith is of one sort to act as Christians whose understanding of the faith is different, ought to know that it is folly to expect our nation to demilitarize

---

6. This treatment of every society as a moral agent and as morally responsible is certainly Biblically justified. Not only is Israel treated thus but also the surrounding nations. (See especially Amos 1–2 as well as the other prophets.) In the Biblical view of man there is no such radical separation of individual from group as we modern individualists like to maintain. (See esp. Pedersen, *Israel, Its Life and Culture*, and Robinson, *Inspiration and Revelation*.) The interpretation of society as a morally responsible agent is also ethically required, inasmuch as the persons we are to love are never really separable from the society of which they are a part (as rationalistic individualists would like to believe), and we cannot, therefore, love the whole person and minister to him without concerning ourselves with the social involvements which are a part of him. A society is after all a new moral unit brought about by the social relationships of persons with each other.

completely. We ought, therefore, to be prepared, along with our negative witness, to support the military bill most in accord with the highest ideals and best moral insights of the total American society. Americans as a whole do not believe in defenselessness or nonresistance, and to demand that they act as if they did, is not only folly, it is positively immoral, for this is to demand that others in our nation live by our faith, our understanding of the will of God, rather than their own. If we would truly be disciples who would love, we must go beyond merely witnessing to our faith, we must concern ourselves with attempting to help our nation come to a deeper understanding of her own faith, her own convictions, the moral insights which are the context in terms of which she lives and acts. And we must attempt to help her come to a decision and work out a course of action in terms of her faith, rather than our own, however much we might desire her to follow what we believe to be the right. [This of course does not mean that our obligation to witness to God's requirement of nonresistant love is in any wise eliminated or even diminished; rather, this points toward the context which we must continuously maintain if that witnessing is truly to be witnessing in love.][7] Any other course than this in the case of the nation of which we are a part—just as in the case of an individual friend—is motivated not so much by real self-giving love as by the desire to dominate and impose our will, the precise opposite of love.

Christian love of the neighbor, then, whether that neighbor be considered as an individual or whether he be viewed collectively as a society, must always have at least these two aspects if it is to be love at all. It must involve a sincere and honest and forthright witness for the truth and the right as God enables us to see the truth and the right. But it must also involve a sincere acceptance of the other as God has given him to us in all his frailties and weaknesses and sin, with the determined effort to help him apprehend more clearly the insights into the truth and the right which God has given him and the effort to help him make the decision in his own free and responsible relation before God.

III

There is also a third aspect of the way in which love expresses itself, and this is in many ways the most difficult and paradoxical of all. If we truly love the other, we cannot forsake him even when he decides in a way

---

7. A later insertion by the author is set off in brackets.

which we take to be wrong and sinful; we must continue to love him as a person and attempt to help him live up to his own insights even when those insights contradict ours. That is to say, we must support him as a person who in the integrity of his own convictions and the depth of his own conscience has come to a decision and is now following out a course of action which we think to be wrong. Again, God's love must be our model. God does not forsake man even when man decides against him and pursues a course of action which is sinful and disobedient. In his faithfulness God continues to love the sinner and seeks to redeem him. The whole Old Testament is the story of God's faithfulness with Israel through all manner of betrayals. Finally, when Israel seems to be a hopeless case, instead of letting her go, God in his love goes beyond anything he has done before and sacrifices of himself. *Agape* is just that which is never stopped by rebuffs, which never gives up: the more impossible the situation, the more effort love expends to redeem the offender. From this point of view the practice of the ban and excommunication (except out of love for the offender) is certainly highly questionable, and the question of church discipline, however necessary it may appear to be, becomes a very difficult issue indeed. We who are imperfect and sinful judges of our neighbor should think long indeed before we cast him out from the community and cease to love and serve him. In such action is our love really the love of God? Is our faithfulness really an expression of his?

We cannot, then, forsake the one who has decided in a manner which we think to be wrong. We must in fact seek to uphold him in his own convictions, even while we are trying to help him come to deeper insight into the implications of the gospel. As Paul points out in the controversy over eating meats offered to idols, even when one is convinced the other is wrong, he has no right to make him violate his conscience, which would be to cause him to sin. "Thus, sinning against your brethren and wounding their conscience when it is weak, you sin against Christ" (1 Cor 8:12; 10:28). This of course does not mean that we are to support all others in everything that they do, for all men, ourselves included, do much out of simple selfishness and sin or plain unconcern, and for this are to be condemned. But it does mean that when we are convinced that the other is acting in accordance with the deepest insights of his conscience, we must support and encourage him in that action. In such a case we certainly have no right to break off fellowship with him. When my friend, then, concludes that it is his Christian duty to join the army, I have no right, on the basis of my own understanding of the Christian gospel, in any way to hinder him from obeying the scruples of his conscience, and thus by my "knowledge" actually to destroy this Christian brother (1 Cor 8:11). Nor is it enough merely to refrain from hindering him. As one who loves his brother, I must do all I can to help and support him in his resolution, to make it possible for him to live according to the insights of his conscience as God has given him those insights. As Christians, after all, our concern is first and foremost with love rather than knowledge. This means that our concern must be for the self-integrity of the person of our fellow before God, in the first place, and only secondly for our own knowledge or understanding of what the Gospel is or implies. We should always beware lest this secondary concern be infected with our own pride in understanding so that in our emphasis on it we have lost the real personal concern of love for our fellow.

This third aspect of love, which goes out to and stays with the one who appears to us to be acting sinfully even in his act of sin, also has important implications for our action as members of a society. The deepest convictions of our society *which is not a Christian society* (in the Mennonite sense of the word) are not fully Christian in character, though they have been influenced by Christian ideals and values. Therefore, we should not expect the course of action which our society follows to be identical with the kind of action which a society of Christians of the Mennonite persuasion might follow. This, however, gives us no leave to withdraw from society and to refuse to participate in its decisions or to support it in the actions to which it is finally led. Nor does this give us leave simply to "witness" to our faith. Rather, if we are truly acting out of love, we must enter into the situation, helping our society come to the best decision of which it is capable in the light of the value insights and ideals carried in the mores, and then support it as best we can in carrying out this decision. Anything less than this would be dogmatic insistence that our society should act according to our knowledge rather than its own, and should exemplify the convictions of our conscience rather than its own. Or, to put it another way, it would involve our expecting our nation to go against its own best knowledge, and if you please, to violate its own conscience. Wounding even the weak conscience of our brethren is a sin against Christ, as Paul reminds us (1 Cor 8:12). As Christians, then, we have no right to withdraw from even the most horribly un-Christian (as it seems to us) decisions which our nation finds itself facing, and we have no right to withdraw from support of the course of action to which it is led, if that action is in accord with the nation's best insights. Instead, we must constantly be attempting to help our nation come to the very best decision of which it is capable (and this will no doubt not be a pacifist decision in the case of war), through not only witnessing to our own understanding of the demands God lays upon us and the nation, but also through helping our nation become more clearly aware of its own highest convictions. This will involve our participating in the actual formulation of policy, for without such participation, our help is only abstract and unreal. The policy which we must help to formulate will not be the kind of policy we might formulate were we acting as members of a Mennonite society; it will be a policy in line with the ideals of the nation in which we are working. To refuse to do this, is to refuse to help our nation to live up to the best that it now knows: it is to refuse to love our neighbor and to assist him in living in moral integrity.

Having aided in the formulation of policy, we must not shy away from also helping to implement it. For this would be to refuse to help our nation stand by its convictions; it would be backing out at just the moment when the greatest support is necessary. This does not mean supporting our nation merely in courses of action with which we happen to agree. It means supporting it in the best courses of action of which it is itself morally capable, and these will include many things with which we disagree, such as, no doubt, a large defense budget. The kind of participation and support which is here envisaged may well require running for Congress and voting "yes" on bills which personally violate one's own convictions; it may require holding office in the State Department (or even the Defense Department), if in such capacity one can really aid one's nation in acting as morally as it is possible for it to act. It does not allow withdrawal from any level of political responsibility simply to keep one's own hands clean, if it is clear that through acting in that position we might help our fellow Americans somehow more nearly to serve Christ's cause—more nearly to act in accordance with the demands which God places upon them—than would otherwise be the case. Our concern must at all points be a concern for helping the nation to come closer to doing what it ought to do, and if this would seem to require great sacrifice on our own part—even the sacrifice of dirtying our hands a little or a great deal—love is always prepared to make whatever sacrifice is required for the sake of the brethren, especially those brethren who are not yet Christian. Our concern for our people as a nation and a society should be so great that we ought to be willing to say with Paul: "For I could wish that I myself were accursed and cut off from Christ for the sake of my brethren, my kinsmen by race" (Rom 9:3). Our love for our fellows should be so great that we should be willing to give up all—even Christ—if this would help to bring them closer to him in understanding and action.

Upon first consideration, it may seem that what is being advocated here is a form of compromise, but this is emphatically not the case. There is no place for compromise in the Christian ethic, if compromise be interpreted as some kind of voluntary sacrifice of the requirements of love to enable action in some other fashion. Love is just that which has adequate resources within itself—the very resources of God himself—to make it possible to meet with and deal with every situation which it confronts in all its variety and all its sinfulness. Without compromising itself at any point, love is able to adapt itself to the needs of every situation it encounters. Love thus never becomes a rigid absolute, the ethical implications of which are clearly and absolutely defined for every situation. This is to turn love into its opposite and to live by law instead of love. Love is just that which has sufficient power in itself to live in openness and freedom and flexibility adapting its response to every situation and to the needs which the situation itself presents[8] without ever losing its own true character as love. It is only a weak defensiveness, unsure of itself and certainly unloving, which is unwilling to face every situation as it comes, and to deal with its needs in terms of those needs themselves, rather than in terms of some pat formula which arbitrarily defines what the needs must be and what the answer to them must be. "The absoluteness of love is its power to go into the concrete situation, to discover what is demanded by the predicament of the concrete to which it turns."[9]

IV

In attempting to deal with the situation in its own terms, love, then, is not compromising itself, but simply being its own true nature, radical, self-giving

---

8. From this point of view, Yoder's contention that "right action can be identical for all" ("Reinhold Niebuhr and Christian Pacifism," 114) is not only so abstract as to be meaningless in understanding the problems of moral decision and action, it is directly counter to the nature of love which always takes account of the concrete needs of the other toward which the action is directed and the situation or context of the action. Since the needs and the situation are different in crucial respects for every decision and action, this statement becomes either a summary of the rigid ethics of law or else a purely formal statement to the effect that right action is always loving action.

9. Tillich, *Systematic Theology*, 1:152.

concern for the neighbor. Such radical concern, as we have seen, must always, in every action, have the neighbor's welfare at heart, it must always be devoted to helping the neighbor achieve morally and religiously the most of which he is capable. This concern, as we have seen, must express itself in at least three aspects simultaneously. Firstly, it is essential that we always try to communicate to the neighbor the best and deepest understanding of the Christian gospel and its implications of which we are capable, i.e., we must "witness" as vigorously, forthrightly, and honestly as we can to our understanding of God's gift and God's demand. This witness must be both in private life and conversation, and through public proclamation and action in the society as a whole. We must do all we can to deepen the insights and elevate the ideals of our neighbor and of the society of which we are a part. Secondly, we must do our utmost to help our neighbor and our nation come to an understanding of the way God is already confronting them in the ideals and values and convictions which are already to some extent honored. We must thus try to help the neighbor see more clearly what his own convictions are and what the implications of those convictions are for the present situation of decision with which he is faced. These convictions will no doubt not be Christian in the sense in which we understand the word, but they are nevertheless the way in which God is now making his demands known to the neighbor through his own conscience. Thirdly, we must encourage and support our neighbor and our nation and help them to follow the course of action most nearly consonant with their best ideals. As members of a democratic society who have the possibility and the responsibility of participating in government, we must do all we can to help the nation act as morally as the present level of its convictions will permit. On the personal level this calls for support of the other in his conscientious decision; on the national level, this calls for participation in the social and political processes whenever and wherever through such participation we might help our nation to act more responsibly to God.

It is of course evident that in any given concrete situation there may well be conflicts between these three aspects of the demands of love upon us. Thus, on a complicated issue like national conscription, a pacifist Christian may have to take what, seen from without, appear to be contradictory positions, but which in reality are an expression of the way in which love seeks the highest possible level of moral activity in every situation. It would certainly be necessary for the pacifist to witness to his convictions about the wrongness and evilness of war. Such witness might express itself in letter writing, in speeches, in refusing to register for the draft, or in a variety of other ways. It must be made clear that the Christian does not rely on force of arms in this world, but on God, even though this lead to a cross, as it did in its most noteworthy exemplification. At the same time, it must be made clear that this nonresistance is not based on any pragmatic conviction that it will win the war or melt the hearts of the enemy or anything else of that sort: it is based on the eschatological conviction at the very heart of Christian faith that the future is in the hands of the God who made himself known in Jesus Christ, and that therefore we can accept whatever that future might bring without regard for ourselves, even though it bring a cross.

But the pacifist Christian cannot stop with this witness. He is well aware of the fact that his nation as a whole and most of the individuals in it do not live by this eschatological faith. They do, however, share certain ideals about justice being better than injustice, about tyranny and slavery being worse than freedom. Though it is of course to be hoped that some might heed the witness of the pacifist Christian, he knows that not many will, and he therefore does not expect the nation as a whole to adopt a policy of defenselessness in the international world, as much as he might desire this. This gives him no justification for withdrawal from the situation, having made his witness. Rather, it means that he must, alongside of his other witness, also help his countrymen to come to an understanding of their own convictions about justice and tyranny as relevant to the problem of conscription. Certainly, a militaristic system in which the burdens are shared as equally as possible among the people is preferable to one which puts the burdens on the helpless or the poor. The pacifist Christian might therefore support through letters, speeches, votes, and so forth, certain military programs as more just and less tyrannical than alternative ones, and certain tax programs for supporting the military as more desirable than others. Were it even possible to secure it, a truly sensitive Christian would not advocate that his nation adopt as policy some such "pacifist" program as unilateral disarmament, for he would know full well that this was not in accord with the convictions of the people, and when the test would come, they would not have the eschatological faith necessary for them to face the cross, but might fall subject to anarchy or tyranny.

The Christian, then, in the second place, must attempt to help the people see and adopt the program most nearly consonant with their convictions. This could conceivably lead to the paradox of a Christian writing to his Congressmen to vote in favor of a given conscription bill as the most adequate for the nation as a whole, but himself finding it necessary to refuse to register under that same bill in order to bear his witness to his deepest Christian convictions. And though he himself be jailed for his non-cooperation with the government's program, he might nevertheless find it necessary to support his country's efforts, e.g., to limit the expansion of Russia, as the best expression of the nation's own convictions at present attainable. Despite the external appearance of contradiction, there is no reason why a pacifist Christian could not hold even the highest offices of his nation during wartime, for his obligation out of love is to [act responsibly in the situation in which he finds God has actually placed him. In this case this means he must] help his people act as morally as they can under the circumstances of war, and he might be more effective in such high office than anywhere else.[10] And yet, at the same time, he would somehow have to make known his conviction that judged by the higher standard of the Christian revelation, which is neither known nor accepted by the nation as a whole, the nation's program is under God's judgment. The Christian does not compromise with love when he is doing his utmost to help his society to act as morally as it can; he compromises with love when he is unwilling to take the risk of being in the world, though not of it, through attempting to withdraw from participation in the social order. Such withdrawal is the worst possible compromise, because it attempts to fulfill the first aspect of love, witnessing, while neglecting the others. Love must find a way to fulfill all three of these aspects in every situation if it is to be the love which is revealed in the New Testament. That this will be exceedingly difficult in nearly every situation, and that different persons and different communities will come to different conclusions about just how this threefold demand is to be met in any given situation, is evident. But this should not surprise Christians, for we know well that even though our knowledge of the situation in which we live and of the gospel itself, as well as our expectations and prophecies about what is to come, is imperfect and must ultimately pass away, nevertheless love will never cease or be destroyed (1 Cor 13:8–13).

Additional Note

A word must be added about certain further theological implications and presuppositions of the position here taken. Yoder has argued for the recognition of a dualistic principle in Christian ethics which takes seriously

---

10. A later insertion by the author is set off in brackets.

the dichotomy between church and world, Christian and non-Christian action.[11] The present essay has tried to take seriously the existence of this dichotomy, but without drawing the conclusion that this implies that the church need not "assume responsibility for the moral structure of non-Christian society."[12] Rather, as God's agent here on earth—the very body of Christ—the church has absolute responsibility for the moral structure and activity of all of the world. There is indeed a dichotomy between church and world, between those who consciously seek to serve Christ, and those who only unconsciously are subject to his lordship.[13] But this dichotomy is not an objective dichotomy the boundaries of which are clearly apparent to Christians; it is not a dichotomy of condemnation through which the church identifies and condemns the world from which it then may separate itself. The parable of the tares (Matt 13:24–30) should remind us that no human eyes are sharp enough to make such distinctions; the separation of the wheat from the tares must await the Last Judgment. This dichotomy is a subjective dichotomy in the consciousness of the Christian. It is a dichotomy of understanding by means of which the Christians and the church are enabled to distinguish and appreciate the difference between the world and themselves and thus be prepared out of love to act in accordance with such distinctions. Instead of providing the basis for a judgment on the world which is forbidden us (Matt 7:1–5), it provides the basis for understanding the world, its actions, and thus dealing with it in love.

This difference in understanding of the meaning of the dichotomy has important theological implications for both the doctrine of man and the doctrine of God. Whereas the *dichotomy of condemnation* can easily betray us into the sin of pride in thinking that we are Christian and hence better than others who are of the world, and thus tends toward breaking down personal relations rather than building them in the manner of love, the *dichotomy of understanding* leads us to see that though there is indeed a true distinction between tares and wheat they are so intermixed in this world, that we must confess that both are in us, i.e., that sin and the world are also present in those of us in the church. (This is certainly the position of the whole New Testament.) Thus, the dichotomy of understanding leads to and is an expression of humility, while the dichotomy of condemnation leads to and is an expression of spiritual pride. We must come to see that the

---

11. Yoder, "Anabaptist Dissent," esp. 50–57.
12. Yoder, "Anabaptist Dissent," 46.
13. Yoder, "Anabaptist Dissent," 54–68.

power structures opposing love, which we as Christians must oppose in the name of love, are not only to be found in the world but also in the church, and particularly in the operation of such practices as the ban and excommunication, where all the social power the community can muster is often directed against the offender, rather than in love for him. Furthermore, we must come to understand that we often unwittingly participate in the power structures of the world with no protest. Thus, as Mennonites, though we have voiced protest against war, we have readily participated in the use of economic power against our employers or employees or competitors with practically no protest at all. Our witness to love has been too exclusively political and military; we have taken the other aspects of social life for granted, and the world is therefore in us. The *dichotomy of understanding* helps us to see that in many ways we are so much a part of each other that the kind of withdrawal presupposed by and advocated by the *dichotomy of condemnation* is not only immoral, but impossible. It does not take due account of the radical solidarity of man, a solidarity presupposed by both the doctrines of the fall in Adam and redemption through Christ.

The *dichotomy of condemnation* leads not only to a false division in man's nature, but to a destruction of the very unity of God. For God is seen as acting in radically different, and even contradictory ways, in relation to man: "in the order of conservation, He uses the violent state to punish evil with evil to preserve a degree of order in society and leave room for His higher working in the order of redemption, through nonresistant self-giving love in Christians."[14] Since God's being and action are inseparable, this kind of dichotomizing makes God into a being of hate and violence as well as love and redemption, a dualism certainly with no New Testament basis, where God reveals himself as *agape*, and a dualism which the doctrine of the Trinity was formulated specifically to overcome. Instead of thus dividing the divine being, it is theologically much more adequate to interpret the different ways in which God deals with men as his loving adaptation of his will to the great variations in man's moral needs, moral insights, and moral capabilities, so that even when God uses the violence of the state—or a revolution against the state for that matter—in his dealings with men, he is doing so out of his love for them. (Cf. Luther's notion of the "strange work" of God's love.) This is certainly the way in which violent and warlike actions attributed to God in the Old Testament are to be understood, and the same holds for God's dealings with man since the

---

14. Yoder, "Anabaptist Dissent," 51.

time of Christ in situations where the revelation of Christ is not known or appropriated, and thus man's situation is analogous to that under the Old Covenant. Thus the different modes of God's relations to and with the church and to and with the world should be understood in terms of God's will to work redemptively in and with both, the differences being due to God's understanding of man's differences, i.e., the differences here also ought to be interpreted in terms of the *dichotomy of understanding* guiding the expression of the divine redemptive love, rather than as an implication of a *dichotomy of condemnation* in which is expressed an opposition between a God of violence and a God of love. If it be said that this view does not take account of God's judgment, that is not true: judgment is certainly involved, e.g., in the way those who face the sword perish by the sword, but it is always essential to understand even such judgment as an expression of the divine redemptive love, which is God's essence.

2

A Second Look at Responsibility

Albert J. Meyer

> Starenstrasse 41
> Basel, Switzerland
> September 10, 1957

Dr. Gordon D. Kaufman
Department of Religion
Pomona College
Claremont, California
USA

Dear Gordon,

John Yoder gave me your paper "Nonresistance and Responsibility" over a year ago, and I have wanted to write to you about it since then. Indeed, I was hoping to get in touch with you before I left the States. I had seen your name several times in National Council correspondence; at my first "Week of Work" everyone wondered if I knew you. In any case, I am sorry for the lateness of this present reply to your article and will be hoping to have the chance to get acquainted with you personally after Mary Ellen and I will have returned to the States in December. If you are interested in corresponding about this before we meet each other—and, before he left for the States, John indicated that this might be the case—I will be eager to have your further comments.

One of the motifs that appears repeatedly in your article is the attack on modern Pharisaism. Where, in Mennonite and other Christian communities, there are an unloving use of social power in the condemnation of offenders in church discipline and an unwitting participation in economic power structures of the world, it must be pointed out that these attitudes are quite out of harmony with self-giving Christian love. I think that criticism of these abuses is appropriate.

I appreciate, too, your frankness in stating some of the problems that arise in the application of your thinking to the sphere of political activity. I feel that your unwillingness to hesitate before conclusions, even when these seem uncomfortably paradoxical, bodes well for our conversation; I hope that my haste in getting immediately to the thinking behind the conclusions with which I would disagree will not appear as a slighting of the importance of our areas of agreement.

In the "Additional Note" appended to your paper you discuss certain theological presuppositions of your position. I would agree with your basic definition of the church-world dichotomy: that it is "between those who consciously seek to serve Christ, and those who only unconsciously are subject to His lordship." It is already clear that the dichotomy is not to be expressed in unconscious worldliness and spiritual pride. Furthermore, although you feel that John Yoder destroys the unity of God in pointing out that God uses the violence of the state to punish evil with evil to preserve a degree of order in society, while he, at the same time, works through the nonresistant love of Christians, I think you will actually find that John is really saying what you are trying to say.[1] One cannot say that God did not condemn Assyria's use of violence against Israel, even though Assyria was "the rod of his anger and the staff of his fury," but God's whole purpose, even in using the evil of those who did now want to consciously follow his will in keeping other evils within bounds, was to show his love even for societies that were not interested in him. God showed his love for Assyria, both in allowing it to use evil and in using even that evil which was not his highest will for holding other evils in check and preventing complete disorder. You, too, point to the fact that God has different modes of relation to and with the church and to and with the world. You and I (and, I think, John) would agree that the dichotomy arises, not from disunity in God, but from the two ways men respond to his call for their allegiance.

You now proceed to define two types of dichotomies without showing how the types are related to each other or to your basic positive definition of church-world dichotomy referred to above. You say the church-world dichotomy is "not an *objective* dichotomy the boundaries of which are

---

1. See for example Yoder, "Wrath of God," and "Le Peuple de Dieu."

clearly apparent to Christians," but that it is "a *subjective* dichotomy in the consciousness of the Christian . . . by means of which the Christian and the church are enabled to distinguish and appreciate the difference between the world and themselves and thus be prepared out of love to act in accordance with such distinctions." What do the words "objective" and "subjective" mean here? Why would an objective dichotomy be more likely to be a dichotomy of condemnation than a subjective one? Since you repeatedly assert that a real dichotomy exists, I am sure you do not mean, by "subjective dichotomy," that Christians are deceiving themselves into believing something that exists only in their consciousnesses. (If the dichotomy existed only in their consciousnesses and nowhere else, one would wonder how it could be a dichotomy of understanding—it would actually be a dichotomy of *misunderstanding* the real world, including the Christian and non-Christian neighbor.)

I think we must face the question: In practical situations, should Christians attempt to make the distinction between the elements of the church-world dichotomy, which we both agree exists, or should they not? I can only agree with the cases you cite to show that Christians should be understanding rather than condemning. But your remarks seem to be more of a corrective than a directive; your emphasis in speaking of excommunication, for example, is on how it should not be done.[2] At times I almost get the impression that you think the Christian had better not try to reckon with the dichotomy in practice at all. This while you clearly indicate in general statements that the point in recognizing the dichotomy in practice is that the Christian is thereby better prepared to deal with the world in love.

I am fully prepared to accept the provisional nature of all human assertions and judgments. This applies to all activities of the church of Christ. If, from the fact that no human eye is sharp enough to make infallible distinctions in church discipline, we would conclude that there should be no attempt at church discipline, we would also have to conclude, from the fact

---

2. For example: "the practice of . . . excommunication (except out of love for the offender) is certainly highly questionable, and the question of church discipline, however necessary it may appear to be, becomes a very difficult issue indeed." I would certainly agree that excommunication should not be considered except out of love for the offender, and that in Mennonite circles the ban is not always practiced out of love. I would wonder, however, if your valid point regarding the dangers in church discipline would not be more convincing for those who are now banning un-Biblically and more constructive for all of us if you would emphasize the way it should be done—or at least clearly say that the necessity for it is not only a matter of appearance. The real question is the one you do not answer: What will this church discipline in love look like?

that all preaching of the word is human activity, that there should be no attempt at preaching.³ The word of God is preached and the proclamation is tested in the congregation in the faith that God will make human words his word; the congregation can only rightly exercise church discipline in submission to God's Spirit as he works in the congregation and in the humble faith that God will act in the congregation's human activity. A congregation's judgment as to the personal faith of a man in another part of the world and not in contact with the congregation could hardly be anything but legalistic, but such caricatures can hardly be considered in a serious discussion of church discipline. Perhaps some Mennonite conference decisions appear to resemble this extreme case. The abuses should then be criticized, but in the knowledge that the church's dealing with the world in love requires the recognition of the dichotomy, not only on the theoretical level, but also in the life of the congregation.

A failure to make the recognized church-world dichotomy a constituent part of your thinking seems to me to crop up repeatedly in the body of your paper. Your scattered remarks on excommunication, used above as an example, are not the most important applications at stake.

To make this clear, I must again insist on the extent of my agreement with you, and especially with the first half of your paper. Certainly, as you say, love must be directed beyond the Christian community. There are several different concepts which can each be considered usefully as types of "responsibility," and it is clear that there is a real, distinctively Christian responsibility for the social order. Love includes witnessing, but it certainly included understanding as well. Christians must respect the "freedom" of sinners to refuse to turn toward God; recognizing the church-world dichotomy in practice involves respecting the freedom of the world to be world.

But already here, in your development, a case in point arises. You explain that, in pastoral counseling, the Christian pacifist would try to help a young man see why he thinks a pacifist position is required of a Christian, but that the counselor could never say, "This is God's will for you," since that would be equivalent to "expecting Christian ethics of the non-Christian." You say that no one has the right to tell a counselee what God requires of him. In a sense, I can understand and agree with everything you say here. But you do not say who the counselee is, and, in view of

3. The danger of partisanship and spiritual pride in preaching is not only hypothetical (Phil 1:15); yet I have never heard of citing the Biblical cases of this to argue that preaching should be discontinued—or even to argue that the church should do less preaching.

the dichotomy, this is important. You come very close to implying that we should not expect Christian ethics of a Christian, and this would indeed be wrong. Further, you object to John's rather general statement that "right action can be identical for all"; you contend that "right action" would depend on concrete needs and the situation, and that these "are different in crucial respects for every decision and action." I do not think that you are as much of an individualist as these words imply.

If Matt 18 was a Swiss Anabaptist definition of the church at a given place, at least they believed that believers in a local congregation had a basis for laying claims on each other in the name of Christ. It seems to me that the import of the New Testament teaching on the congregation is that, although needs and situations vary, the differences are not really as crucial as the unity of the members in Christ. In this way, there is, at least on the local level, such a thing as Christian ethics, an ethics revealed by the Spirit in the congregation, that can be expected of the local Christians. Speaking in terms of the alternatives you mention, this ethic could be identical for all (on many matters, of course, the congregation would feel that it would not be identical for all; that would still be a voice of the congregation), and it would be neither a "rigid ethics of law" nor "a purely formal statement to the effect that right action is always loving action." Instead it would be truly an ethic for the situation.

If we agree on the possibility of conversation in the congregation and that saying "love includes understanding" is not an attempt to modify this possibility, I would agree with your emphasis on this point. This applies to social groups as well as to individuals, since, as you point out, not only the church, but every social group, is a morally and religiously responsible agent.[4]

The deepest problem in your paper arises when you discuss the third aspect of love: supporting the individual or society even when we think he or it is wrong. You consistently talk about "every social group," "every society," and "a society" until you get to the discussion of the third aspect of love.[5] Then, in the middle of the paragraph, it seems that the basic character

---

4. Your comment on the ambiguity of the concept of responsibility is applicable here as well. You say that responsibility for Christians is distinctive in that it "derives more directly and more decisively from God's action as redeemer, from God's action in Jesus Christ." The moral and religious responsibility of non-Christian social groups that have not the freedom of redemption in Christ will naturally be different from the church's responsibility in certain important ways, too.

5. "This third aspect of love . . . also has important implications for our action as

of the church-world dichotomy is completely lost from the structure of your reasoning. You suddenly start talking about "our society which is not a Christian society": in one sentence you overlook our membership in all but one of the societies to which each of us belongs, and the one society you choose to consider further happens not to be the church. Earlier you had indicated that the mores of a community may be quite at variance from those of other peoples.[6] And you had singled out "the total American society," "our nation," and "the nation of which we are a part" for special attention in your discussion of the second aspect of love. Now you talk of the nation as "our society," apply what Paul said about more scrupulous brothers in Christ to say we should support our fellow citizens right or wrong,[7] and say that, when in a given situation we have to decide whether to act as citizens or as Mennonites, we should act as citizens first.[8] Obviously we should not act as though there were nothing but Mennonites in the world. At one point, you rightly recognize the fact that we are members of a Mennonite society and of a national society—and we are members of various family, community, regional, and other international societies, as well. But, although you and I would no doubt agree theoretically on the importance of the church-world dichotomy, here, in practice, and specifically in the examples you use, you imply an American/non-American dichotomy. Here in the case where it makes a difference, the church-world dichotomy seems to have been sloughed off as a pious, but irrelevant, formula.

---

members of a society. The deepest convictions of our society *which is not a Christian society*" (italics yours). Further: "we should not expect the course of action which our society follows to be identical with the kind of action which a society of Christians of the Mennonite persuasion might follow. This, however, gives us no leave to withdraw from society and to refuse to participate in its decision or to support it in the actions to which it is finally led."

6. "The actions of our nation, as of all nations, result . . . also from the context of moral values and insights carried and kept alive in the mores, customs and laws of the country. . . . This context is of course never precisely definable, nor is it the same in all parts of the community. The mores of the deep South are somewhat different from the North on the matter of relations between the races, and the mores of one small homogeneous community, e.g., the Hutterites, may be quite at variance from those of the surrounding peoples."

7. For example, your use of 1 Cor 8:12: "Thus, sinning against your brethren and wounding their conscience when it is weak, you sin against Christ" in your discussion of third aspect of love.

8. "The policy which we must help to formulate will not be the kind of policy we might formulate were we acting as members of a Mennonite society; it will be a policy in line with the ideals of the nation in which we are working."

PART I: ON CHRISTIAN RESPONSIBILITY IN AND FOR THE "WORLD"

The fact is that the Christian is not a member of one society that is characterized by the continued presence of sin; social problems are so complex precisely because the collective situation in which the Christian finds himself involves the presence of a number of social groups, each with its own norms and ideals, with some of the ideals and norms of one group in radical conflict with those of the other groups. Saying that the individual in this situation should "support" each group may be true, as a vague indication, but it evades the real question: Which of the societies has the priority when their ideals conflict?

To a European Christian reading your paper, the conflict is immediately obvious. All you say about "supporting our nation," "including . . . a large defense budget," "the Defense Department," and "help our fellow Americans" actually sounds dangerously nationalistic to someone on the other side. You said that the self-giving of the Christian community should not be directed largely to members of that community; it is now no solution to conclude that the self-giving of Christians should be directed instead to the nation. You cannot be on all sides at once—at least not by picking the American nation as the object of your first loyalty.

The real conflict is not between the three aspects of the demands of love upon the individual, but between the different societies that claim his support. It seems to me that the whole point of the church-world dichotomy is that, in this complex of societies, the Christian declares that he is willing to make an open commitment and to take sides, even if that means a certain unavoidable separation from all societies but that unique society, the church of Christ. The Christian makes this decision because he is convinced that it is precisely in this "separation from the world" that he can best fulfill his "real Christian responsibility for the social order."

My reaction to what appears to me to be a failure to consider the acknowledged dichotomy in practice can be expressed in another way. You clearly indicate that the goal of Christian social action is not keeping one's own hands clean, but "helping our fellow Americans somehow more nearly to serve Christ's cause."[9] You have earlier implied that our national society is not a Christian society. Assuming that you are not interested in simply applying Christian ethics to non-Christians, I must ask whether your suggested

---

9. "It does not allow withdrawal from any level of political responsibility simply to keep one's own hands clean, if it is clear that through acting in that position we might help our fellow Americans somehow more nearly to serve Christ's cause, more nearly to act in accordance with the demands which God places upon them, than would otherwise be the case."

participation in the State Department or Defense Department would be appropriate for reaching the goal you set forth: Will it "help our fellow Americans somehow more nearly to serve Christ's cause"? It is clear that the advocates of the medieval *corpus christianum* and modern proponents of the *eglise multitudiniste* form of the church would reply in the affirmative. However, besides the theological fact that Christ did not attempt to influence and demonstrate his solidarity with society by paradoxically cooperating in the sinning of people around him, but by allowing men to have him put to death as a traitor, I wonder if you would not agree that, historically, the countries with a mass-church mentality have not demonstrated a "more Christian" standard of public ethics, to say nothing of their failure to bring greater percentages of their populations to practicing Christianity. I would think the best way for reaching the goal you state is for the church to be the church. Only when Christians realize that the dichotomy means that Christian ethics does apply to Christians do they see how dirty their hands really are; only to the extent that they fully and consciously and practically acknowledge Christ's lordship and all the distinctiveness that it may imply will their unbelieving fellow citizens see the body of the One they are more nearly to serve.

"Love" is no longer Christian love when it is supporting every neighbor in terms of his own understanding or misunderstanding. Christian love is treating every neighbor as Christ would treat him. I agree with your statement that "love is not a 'thing.'" But love is more than just "a relationship"; it is a unique kind of relationship. Love goes to the heart of evil situations, but it enters in a distinctive way. It is possible to enter evil situations in such a way that the evil is made worse. Christ was killed, not for understanding and supporting his nation, but for bringing into his relationships with individuals and social groups, and even into the most evil situations, a most distinctive kind of love. Indeed, his love looked more like a judgment than a blessing to those who opposed him; it seemed impossible to be on both sides of the fence with respect to him. Whether our love will look more like witnessing, understanding, or supporting, and whether it can look like all three at once, will depend on the situation. But this is sure: it will have some of the same distinctiveness which in Christ's situation was answered by separation and hatred. "The servant is not greater than his lord."

Sincerely,

Albert J. Meyer

3

Nonresistance and Responsibility

A Critical Analysis

David Habegger

Gordon Kaufman's article "Nonresistance and Responsibility" is addressed to a weakness of contemporary Mennonitism. His is a vital concern. As Mennonites we have drawn a clear line between the church and the world, and this has been necessary. But beyond this we need to examine what it means to witness to, to redeem, and to love the world. Kaufman calls us to grapple with the problem of relating ourselves to the society around us in a truly Christian and loving manner. We have isolated ourselves from the rest of the world to too great an extent.

Yet we must take care not to lose ground in one area as we explore another. Kaufman's concern for the need to approach our fellow men in love, even as Christ loved us, is valid; and we must accept what he says as a just rebuke. Yet he seems to have been led by this concern to conclusions which we find wanting when measured by the Spirit of God as revealed in Jesus Christ.

A study of his paper raises questions at several points, but the central issue is his discussion of what it means to love. Several excellent statements about love are made in the paper, but in viewing the total picture one comes to sense an important lack which undermines much of what Kaufman has said. That lack is the failure to see that love is righteous.

Love Is Righteous

We would agree with the statement, "Christian love, as perfectly exemplified in God's act in Christ, sacrifices itself for and to sin; Christian love gives itself to its own enemies."[1] We can also subscribe with some reservations to the statement that "love goes to the very heart of the most sinful situations that it can find, and there it gives of itself without any reservation whatever."[2] But his reasoning leads us to the conclusion that to be truly loving would mean that Christians should "support the military bill most in accord with the highest ideals and the best moral insights of the total American society" or that we should encourage and individual to "live up to his own insights even when these insights contradict ours."[3] Thus he seems to have read into his understanding of love, elements irreconcilable with the demands of Jesus Christ.

We would agree with Gordon Kaufman that love is not just another principle to add to the set of principles by which men in general live. It is the first and greatest command. Yet when we say that we must obey love and love alone, we can go far astray. We must affirm that love is not antinomian unbound by any law. While the Christian life is certainly not lived in blind obedience to commandments, on the other hand we cannot say that the commandments may be disregarded. In a very real sense the commandments are retained, though insofar as men are truly Christian, they should not need them—being so driven by the love of Christ that they do not seek to kill to steal, or to dishonor their parents.

The love which seeks to support men in whatever they decide could easily become nothing more than the love of a grandfather. Rather we must love as do responsible parents, who realize that children must take medicine when they are ill even if they dislike medicine. Righteousness without love is unredemptive, but love without righteousness is mere sentimentality.

Kaufman writes categorically, "We cannot, then, forsake the one who has decided in a manner which we think wrong." Yet a few sentences later he adds, "This of course does not mean that we are to support all others in everything that they do, for all men, ourselves included, do much out of simple selfishness and sin or plain unconcern, and for this are to be

---

1. Kaufman, "Nonresistance," essay in this volume, 6.
2. Kaufman, "Nonresistance," essay in this volume, 6.
3. Kaufman, "Nonresistance," essay in this volume, 14.

condemned."[4] How are these statements to be reconciled? What does it mean "not to support"—to "condemn" those who act out of sin? Is no moral judgment involved? How does one determine when his neighbor is committing a wrong action out of selfishness and when he is doing it according to his best insights?

Apart from the exceptional statement just referred to, it would seem that, in general, Kaufman so separates love and justice that love becomes amoral. If I understand correctly, he would affirm that Jesus Christ himself can be said to have sinned.[5] Under Jewish legalism as taught by the Pharisees, Jesus was of course a sinner, but the Biblical testimony is to the effect that Jesus was without sin. This does not mean that Jesus was living a libertinistic life where no moral standards were held valid. Rather, his was a higher righteousness. He was made to be sin only in a substitutionary sacrificial sense. He alone of all men could truly say he kept the commandments.

We must therefore affirm that the Christian who "supports the military bill most in accord with the highest ideals and best moral insights of the total American society"[6] is not truly loving, though the surrounding society might approve such an attitude and call it love. "Love" tailored to fit society's wishes is at variance with righteousness. Granted, one can be so self-righteous as to become unloving; yet to be so "loving" as to become unrighteous is no better.

It is further striking how Kaufman has in effect limited "love" to the borders of the United States. To support the military bill in line with the highest American ideals is to love Americans more than Russians or Chinese, thus denying on the most universal level the very human solidarity which he began by affirming. Thus, in spite of the initial emphasis on self-giving, the argument concludes by supporting national self-interest. It is in situations such as this that righteousness helps "love" overcome its nearsightedness and natural self-seeking inclinations.

---

4. Kaufman, "Nonresistance," essay in this volume, 14.

5. Kaufman, "Nonresistance," essay in this volume, 6. This conclusion seems to be dictated by the context in which 2 Cor 5:21 is related to "self-giving to the evils of the sinful situation."

6. Kaufman, "Nonresistance," essay in this volume, 13.

The Relativity of Truth

Kaufman criticizes Yoder's statement that there is a possibility of defining a right action which would be identical for all.[7] He probably would likewise reject the more qualified Statement of this position, with which I fully agree: "Here the sectarian believes that with the Holy Spirit's help the congregation can deduce from the New Testament a set of instructions, commands, and prohibitions, which are objectively valid in that they translate the will of God adequately for all Christians at a given time and place."[8] By considering all men's best insights as valid, as long as they are sincere the Christian is able to follow contradictory patterns of action. Gordon Kaufman would like to call this situation paradoxical but neither side of a valid paradox can be contradictory to the nature of God or his revelation.

The effect of making truth relative to the individual is to undercut the prophetic witness. In the following sentence there are several ideas. "But surely no one has the right to say to the other: 'This is what you must decide, this is God's will for you.'" We might agree that we cannot tell others, "This is what you must do." Yet we are responsible to tell them, "This is what you ought to do." This is the will of God for you" is just what Paul told those to whom he wrote (1 Thess 5: 18). That "no one else has the right to play the role of the mediator and tell him what God requires of him" is simply not biblical. The man of God has not only every right but in fact the responsibility to tell others of God's requirements (Mic 6:8). Jesus himself said, "As my Father hath sent me, even so send I you" (John 20:21; cf. 17:18). Paul's letters all close with instructions telling people what they ought to do. To tell another what he ought to do is not necessarily seeking to dominate him. It may be the effort of love to bring him into the love and will of God. Of course, this experience may be frustrating to the one whose self-seeking life or whose improper effort to serve God it interferes with. But such frustration is a part of the process of helping him "to be the responsible and free person whom God had created him to be." So to speak is not "to demand that a man decide and live by a faith which is not his own," but rather to invite one to accept and to live by the Christian faith as his own.

It is not clear just what moral guidance Gordon Kaufman's approach would actually give in a concrete situation. On the one hand he gives token

---

7. Kaufman, "Nonresistance," essay in this volume, 17.
8. Yoder, "Anabaptist Dissent," 61.

recognition to the rightness of pacifism.⁹ He says that the Christian may find "himself jailed for his non-cooperation with the government's program." On the other hand, he at once maintains the possibility of his serving the state by leading his nation in time of war. Is this a rational possibility? Could a judge condemn himself to jail for nonregistration? Can we witness both for and against an armaments bill at the same time? Have we not here a menace of moral schizophrenia, not only disastrous for the individual but ludicrous to those who hear? "The first aspect of our responsibility to our fellow men is, then, so to live and speak so that we witness to God's love for man."[10] Truly life and word must be a unity. "But we keep trying to divide the two into a word-ministry and a work-ministry and often even put a premium on one or the other. When we split the two we crush the power of the Gospel and the Word of God becomes bound."[11] Yet is not Kaufman telling us to do one thing and say another?[12]

The paper's constant emphasis on the validity of the non-Christian's moral insights and on the integrity of his person is too dominant. Of course, God does not leave himself without a witness to any man, and we should violate no one's integrity. Yet neither should we affirm the sufficiency of "integrity" for man apart from God. We take a dim view both of his capacity to know the good and of his ability to do the good he knows. The redemption he needs is more than living up to his best insights. The brotherhood which binds us as sinners to the unregenerate world—a true enough point in its place—is overemphasized at the expense of the brotherhood of the redeemed, as Albert Meyer has already argued. The cleavage between the church and the world is barely discernible. Yet it was the church that Christ came to establish, for which he died, and in which he is best seen speaking. Any statement which so minimizes the church that revelation has little more meaning within the fellowship than without is suspect.

---

9. "The Christian does not rely on force of arms in this world, but on God, even though this lead to a cross" (Kaufman "Nonresistance," essay in this volume, 19).

10. Kaufmnn "Nonresistance," essay in this volume, 8.

11. Enz, "Biblical Imperative," 4.

12. This is especially the case in the later bracketed insertion "This of course does not mean that our obligation to witness to God's requirement of nonresistant love is in any wise eliminated or even diminished; rather, this points toward the context which we must continuously maintain if that witnessing is truly to be witnessing in love." See Kaufman, "Nonresistance," essay in this volume, 13.

Our Responsibility

"Nonresistance and Responsibility" claims that our sole duty is to love absolutely and without reservation. Is this actually the case? Is love not a means to attain our goal, rather than the goal itself? Our goal is to redeem men, bringing them into the presence of Christ and the fellowship of his church. The first and last requirement is to witness by word and deed, in love, to this end. Men outside the fellowship of Christ are men in sin, needing a Savior. We attribute no eternal value to men's insights and strivings as long as they avoid the question of their relation to God. We acknowledge that Christians too are sinners, but they are sinners saved by grace and therefore saints striving after holiness. To encourage the world in its efforts outside of Christ is not to be redemptive but rather to assist the world in its rebellion against God.

I therefore have reservations about the statement that "love must always be understood as just that which never retreats from an evil situation, but always advances into it totally without any regard for itself."[13] It would be true to say that the Christian should never retreat from a given situation for selfish reasons; yet he should seek to be redemptive in the best way possible. God chose a particular time and place to send his Son into the world. His love was wise; it took into consideration the possibilities of reception and response and the opportunities for the growth of the church. Jesus carefully chose the times and places for his working. There were many hungry and sick in his day; yet there were times when he retreated from them to fulfill a greater purpose. At every point love must survey its resources and evaluate how they are best to be expended. This is the truth which the statement quoted above fails to recognize. To say that the Christian should love everyone is meaningless. What we mean is that as Christians we must love anyone, especially the unfortunate and sinful. But no individual can possibly enter every sinful situation that confronts him. The good Samaritan was not asked to travel daily the road to Jericho to pick up those who might have been way laid. This need to measure and allocate one's resources—and not any relativity of truth—is the reason love is not codifiable. "How much should I love?" is not the question. In theory love may know no bounds, but in application we must relate it to the individual and the congregation. Our obligations differ. It would be the height of legalism to say that we must not retreat from any situation.

---

13. Kaufman, "Nonresistance," essay in this volume, 5.

PART I: ON CHRISTIAN RESPONSIBILITY IN AND FOR THE "WORLD"

We must challenge the acceptance of a secular definition of responsibility. In the eyes of most of his contemporaries Jesus did not appear to be "responsible" or "relevant," nor does the world see him any differently today. Yet his total obedience was both responsible and relevant. The work of Paul and the early church appeared to be missing the issues of the day when viewed through the eyes of the Roman authorities; yet this service was the most responsible of all, and those who thought otherwise brought the empire down on their heads.

"In the ancient polytheisms the chief aim of worship was so to integrate man within his society and society within nature that the whole would be borne along in a cosmic and gentle rhythm. Biblical man had no such confidence in the eternity of either society or nature. The world is in all of its aspects a 'fallen' world."[14] What was the chief aim of polytheism is also the chief aim of modern psychiatry and sociology. Has Gordon Kaufman somehow sought to bring this idea into a Christian framework with his view of an unqualified "love" which supports men in their best intentions? Our mission as individuals and churches is to uphold before our nation and all nations the "ought" of God over against the "is" of society, as we seek to fulfill the demands of the Great Commission.

I am grateful for Gordon Kaufman's willingness to state and to discuss his views openly. His intention, as noted at the outset, is a corrective one. He speaks to a weakness of Mennonite churches and therefore emphasizes, purposely and justifiably, the needs he hopes to help correct. Yet his picture of the Mennonite Church is not the one I see. Despite our many weaknesses, there are many who are seriously striving to love as Christ loved. There have been cases of unloving excommunication, but many members have been dealt with redemptively. The representatives sent before governments have not to my knowledge advocated that the nation disarm unilaterally. In our mission work we have sought to minister to the whole man and are not satisfied merely to shout a witness from a distance. We have much to learn, but let us recognize in the Mennonite churches the church of Jesus Christ and believe that there are still "seven thousand . . . which have not bowed unto Baal." May our common search for the path of faithfulness continue.

---

14. Wright, *Biblical Doctrine*, 35.

4

The Otherness of the Church

John Howard Yoder

That the "Constantinian era" is coming to an end has become one of the commonplaces of Occidental social analysis. The fact that this breakdown has at some points been anticipated in North America (in the disestablishment of religion) and at other points is evolving differently here (rising church membership) hides from no one the fact that the framework of thought about the church, the world, and their mutual interrelations, which for centuries was shared by all "mainline" Christian theologies, Protestant and Catholic, orthodox and rationalist, has fallen away in the last two generations. The assumption that we live in a Christian world no longer holds.

The predominant theological response to this development has been to note the fact without evaluating it. Apart from a few clericalists and monarchists who are still working to restore the past, most thinkers simply make their peace with the new situation as they had with the old, assuming that the total process must somehow be of God's doing. For the first three centuries Christians were persecuted by the world; that was as it had to be. For over a millennium Christians ruled the world; that was as it should be. In the modern age the world again faces the church as an autonomous, articulate, partly hostile party; that is as it should be. The Lord gave; the Lord takes away; blessed be the name of the Lord. The early church was right in facing persecution courageously; the church of the fourth century was right in making her peace with the world; the churches of the Middle Ages and the Reformation were right in leaning on the state; and now that that is no longer possible, the church is again right in "making the best of a bad deal" and striking out on her own.

But we can no longer so simply identify the course of history with Providence. We have learned that history reveals as much of Antichrist as of Christ. We are no longer sure that we are edging upward at the top of a progression of which every preceding step must have been right for its time, since it led us to this pinnacle. Above all we have learned to ask if it can really be the will of the Lord of history that his church should be limping after history, always attempting to adapt to a new situation which she assumes to be providential, always a half step behind in the effort to conform, being made by history instead of making history. We can therefore not say whether the de-Constantinizing of the church—be it in the form or possible disestablishment in East Germany, in that of defecting membership in Western Europe, or in the more complex forms taken by post-Christian paganism elsewhere—is a bane or a boon, until we have sought on a deeper level an understanding of the roots of modern secularism, of the *Mündigkeit*, the coming-of-age of the world. In this search we shall expect no new answers but shall attempt to illuminate some old answers with a modified question. We begin by seeking to isolate the concepts "church" and "world" in their pre-Constantinian significance. "World" (*aion houtos* in Paul, *kosmos* in John) signifies in this connection not creation or nature or the universe, but rather the fallen form of the same, no longer conformed to the divine creative intent. The state, which for present purposes may be considered as typical for the world, belongs with the other *exousiae* in this realm. Over against this "world" the church is visible; identified by baptism, the Lord's supper, discipline, morality, and martyrdom. It is self-evident for the early centuries, as a part of this visibility of the fellowship of disciples, that the church's members do not normally belong in the service of the world and *a fortiori* in that of the pagan state.

But behind or above this visible dichotomy there is a believed unity. All evidence to the contrary notwithstanding, the church of the New Testament believed that her Lord was also Lord over the world. The explicit paganism of state, art, economics, and learning did not keep her from confessing their subordination to him who sitteth at the right hand of God. This belief in Christ's lordship over the *exousiae* enabled the church, in and in spite of her distinctness from the world, to speak to the world in God's name, not only in evangelism, but in ethical judgment as well. She could take on a prophetic responsibility for civil ethics without baptizing the state or the statesman. The justice she demanded of the state was not Christian righteousness but human *justitia*; this she could demand from pagans, not because of any belief in a universal innate moral sense' but because of her faith in her Lord. Thus, the visible distinctness of church and world was not an insouciant irresponsibility; it was a particular, structurally appropriate way, and the most effective way, for Christians to be responsible for the larger society.

This attitude was meaningful for the church because she believed that the state was not the ultimately determinative force in history. She ascribed to the state at best a preservative function in the midst of an essentially rebellious world, whereas the true sense of history was to be sought elsewhere, namely, in the work of the church. This high estimation of her own vocation explains both her visible distinctness from the world and the demands she addressed to it. The depth of her conviction that her own task was the most necessary enabled her to leave other functions in society to pagans; her faith in Christ's lordship enabled her to do so without feeling that she was abandoning them to Satan.

It follows from the "already, but not yet" nature of Christ's lordship over the powers that there is no one tangible, definable quantity which we can call "world." The *aion houtos* is at the same time a kingdom and a chaos. The "world" of politics, the "world" of economics, the "world" of the theater, the "world" of sports, the under "world," and a host of others—each is a demonic blend of order and revolt. The world "as such" has no intrinsic ontological dignity. It is creaturely order in the state of rebellion; rebellion is, however, for the creature estrangement from what it "really is"; therefore, we cannot ask what the world "really is," somehow "in itself." This observation is borne out by the New Testament's use of a multiplicity of terms, most of them in the plural—principalities, powers, thrones, archangels, dominions—when speaking of the world. All that the powers have in common is their revolt, and revolt is not a principle of unity. Since the prince of the power of the air is a liar from the beginning, he cannot even lie consistently. Only the hidden lordship of Christ holds this chaos of idolatrous "worlds" together.

We have seen that for the early Christians, church and world were visibly distinct, yet affirmed in faith to love one and the same Lord. This pair of affirmations is what the so-called Constantinian transformation changes (we here use the name of Constantine merely as a label for this transformation, which began before AD 200 and took over two hundred years; the use of his name as a label does not involve an evaluation of Constantine's person or work). The most pertinent fact about the new state of things after Constantine and Augustine is not that Christians were no longer persecuted and began to be privileged, nor that emperors built churches and presided over ecumenical deliberations about the Trinity; what matters is that the two visible realities, church and world, were fused. There is no longer anything to call "world"; state, economy, art, rhetoric, superstition, and war have all been baptized.

It is not always recognized in what structural connection this change, in itself self-evident, stands to a new distinction which now arose. It was perfectly clear to men like Augustine that the world had not become Christian through its compulsory baptism. As a result, there sprang up the doctrine of the invisibility of the true church, in order to permit the affirmation that on some level, somewhere the difference between belief and unbelief, i.e., between church and world, still existed. But this distinction had become invisible, like faith itself. Previously Christians had known as a fact of experience that the church existed but had to believe against appearances that Christ ruled over the world. After Constantine one knew as a fact of experience that Christ was ruling over the world, but had to believe against the evidence that there existed a believing church. Thus, the order of redemption was subordinated to that of preservation, and the Christian hope turned inside out.

The practical outworkings of this reversal were unavoidable. Since the church has been filled with people in whom repentance and faith, the presuppositions of discipleship, are absent, the ethical requirements set by the church must be adapted to the achievement level of respectable unbelief. Yet a more significant reason for moral dilution lies in the other direction. The statesman, who a century earlier would have been proud to declare that his profession was unchristian by nature, now wants to be told the opposite. What he does is the same as before, if not worse. Yet since there are no more heathen to do the work (correction: of course there are heathen; everyone knows, with Augustine, that most of the population is unbelieving, but unbelief has become invisible, like the church), since there are no more confessing heathen, every profession must be declared Christian. Since Christian norms for the exercise of some professions are difficult to find, the norms of pagan *justitia* will be declared to define the content of Christian love. The autonomy of the state and of the other realms of culture is not brought concretely under the lordship of Christ, with the total revision of form and content which that would involve; it has been baptized while retaining its former content. An excellent example is Ambrose's rephrasing of Cicero's political ethics.

And yet the medieval church maintained significant elements of otherness in structure and in piety, which are generally underestimated. When under the influence of men like Troeltsch we speak of the "medieval synthesis" and of a fusion of church and world such that the salt had lost all its savor, the risk of caricature is great. Whatever was wrong with the basic confusion we have just described, the church in the Middle Ages retained her consciousness of her distinctness from the world. The higher level of morality asked of the clergy, the international character of the hierarchy, the visibility of the hierarchy in opposition to the princes, the gradual moral education of barbarians into monogamy and legality, foreign mission, apocalypticism, and mysticism—all of these preserved an awareness, however distorted and polluted, of the strangeness of God's people in a rebellious world. Will the Reformation unearth and fan into new flame these smoldering coals, or will it bury them for good?

Despite many insights and initiatives which could have led in another direction, the Reformation, deciding between 1522 and 1525 in favor of political conservatism, decided at the same time not to challenge the Constantinian compromise. The Reformers knew very well of the "fall of the church"; but they dated this fall not in the fourth century but rather in the sixth and seventh. They did not see that the signs of fallenness to which they objected—papacy, Pelagianism, hagiolatry, sacramentalism—were largely fruits of the earlier confusion of church and world. For this reason, there remains a fundamental inconsistency in the work of the Reformers. They decided in favor of the Middle Ages. They wanted nothing other than the renewal and purification of the *Corpus Christianum*. And yet they were driven, for reasons partly of tactics, partly of principle, to shatter that unity which they sought to restore. We have already noted that the hierarchy, the higher ethical commitment of the orders, and the missionary and international character of the Roman Church had preserved, even though in a distorted form, a residual awareness of the visible otherness of the church. All of these dimensions of specificity were abandoned by the Reformation.

In the face of monasticism, the Reformation affirmed the ethical value of the secular vocation. Through the imprecision of their terms this affirmation, right in itself, amounted to the claim, as wrong as the intention was right, that every calling is its own norm, thereby heightening immeasurably (and unintentionally) the autonomy of the several realms of culture. Proper behavior in a given vocation is decided in post-Reformation ethics not by Christ but by the inherent norms of the vocation itself, known by reason, from creation, despite the fall. The Reformers did not intend thereby to secularize the vocations and declare the order of creation independent of Christ; this is demonstrated by their continued efforts to give instructions to statesmen and by their claim that certain professions are unchristian (not those of prince, mercenary, and hangman, but those of monk, usurer, and prostitute); nevertheless the autonomy of state and vocation was mightily furthered by what they said, so that even today many German Lutherans will argue that faithfulness to Luther demands that they let the state be master in its own house.

When the church of the fourth century wished to honor Constantine, she interpreted him in the light of her eschatology. For Eusebius the Christian *Imperator* stood immediately under *Christos Pantokrator*; the state was unequivocally taken up into the realm of redemption. The Reformation, however, placed the state in the realm of creation. Theoretically this meant decreasing the state's dignity; practically it meant increasing its autonomy. The prince in the sixteenth century is a Christian, the noblest and most honored member of the church; but the work he does as prince is a purely rational one, finding its norms not in Christ but in the divinely fixed structure of society; it is a work a reasonable Turk could do as well.

Further, the Reformers did not call on the state abstractly, on the state "as such," or on the state universal (Charles V), but on the territorial state—on the Elector of Saxony and Milords of Zürich—to carry through the Reformation in God's name. The territorial state was thereby loosed from the network of imponderable political and ecclesiastical forces and counterforces which in their complex entirety had formed and held together the *Corpus Christianum*, and given an immediate, unequivocal, uncontrollable divine imperative, subject to no higher earthly authority. Previously political action in God's name had been possible only in the name of the church universal; now religiously motivated political struggle is possible between Christian peoples. The Thirty Years' War was the last crusade—on both sides.

The conviction that the center of the meaning of history is in the work of the church, which had been central in the pre-Constantinian church and remained half alive in the Middle Ages, is now expressly rejected. The prince is not only a Christian, not only a prominent Christian; he is now the bishop. True faith and the true church being invisible, the only valid aims of effort in the visible world are those which take the total secular society of a given area as the object of responsibility. The prince wields not only the sword, but all other powers as well. The church confesses in deed and sometimes in word that not she, but the state, has the last word and incarnates the ultimate values in God's work in the world. What is called "church" is an administrative branch of the state on the same level with the army or the post office. Church discipline is applied in Zürich, Bern, and Geneva by the civil courts and police. It is assumed that there is nothing wrong with this since the true church, being invisible, is not affected. It cannot be said that this turn of events was desired by the Reformers. Their uniform intention was a renewal of the visible, faithful fellowship of believers. But the forces to which they appealed for support, namely, the drives toward autonomy which exist in the state and the other realms of culture, were too strong to be controlled once they had been let loose.

In the context in which the Reformers made this decision there is much that we can understand and even approve of. Their faith in the all-powerful word, which will not return void if it but be rightly preached, and their awareness of the divine ordination of the secular order, which were their conscious points of departure, were true in themselves. But they did not succeed in bringing up for examination the Constantinian synthesis itself. Thus their decisions, which in their minds were consistently conservative, reveal themselves in a broader socio-historical perspective to have been inconsistent and revolutionary. The order of creation, in which they placed the state and the vocations, could with a turn of the hand become the deistic order of nature or the atheistic order of reason without any change in its inner structure. The right of the local government to administer the church in the interest of the Reformation could become a right of the state to use the church for its own purposes, and there was no court of appeal. The divine obligation of Zürich or Saxony to shatter the superstructure of the Holy Roman Empire could flip over—especially after the Thirty Years' War badly discredited confessionalism as a moral imperative—and appear as the absolute *raison d'etat*. It was therefore precisely the attempt of the Reformers to maintain the medieval ideal and to lay claim on the autonomous dynamics of state and profession which led to the secularization characteristic of the modern period. Fully to accept the Constantinian synthesis is to explode it. The Reformers created modern secularism; not, as the liberalism of two generations ago boasted, intentionally, by glorifying the individual, but unintentionally, through the inner contradictions of their conservatism.

The Constantinian approach has thereby shown itself to be incapable, not accidentally, but constitutionally, of making visible Christ's lordship over church and world. The attempt to reverse the New Testament relationship of church and world, making faith invisible and making the Christianization of the world a historic achievement within institutional forms, was undertaken in good faith, but has backfired, having had the sole effect of raising the autonomy of unbelief to a higher power. Islam, Marxism, secular Humanism, and Fascism—in short, all the major adversaries of Christian faith in the Occident and the strongest adversaries in the Orient as well—are not nature, or culture, religions, but hybrid faiths, all of them the progeny of Christianity's infidelity, of the spiritual miscegenation involved in trying to make a culture-religion out of faith in Jesus Christ. As religious adversaries in our day, these hybrid faiths are more formidable than any of the pagan alternatives faced by Paul, by Francis Xavier, or by Livingstone. He who has refused to learn from the New Testament must now learn from history; the church's responsibility to and for the world is first and always to be the church. The short-circuited means used to "Christianize" "responsibly" the world in some easier way than by the gospel have a bad effect of dechristianizing the Occident and demonizing paganism.

What then should be the path of the church in our time? We must first of all confess—if we believe it—that the meaning of history lies not in the acquisition and defense of the culture and the freedoms of the West, not in the aggrandizement of material comforts and political sovereignty, but in the calling together of "men for God from every tribe and tongue and people and nation," a "people of his own who are zealous for good deeds." The basic theological issue is not between right and left, not between Bultmann and Barth, not between the sacramental and the prophetic emphases, nor between the Hebraic and Greek mentalities, but between those for whom the church is a reality and those for whom she is the institutional reflection of the good and bad conscience, of the insights, the self-encouragement—in short, of the religion of a society.

If with the apostles we confess the Holy Spirit and the church, we must further recognize that unbelief also incarnates itself. The "world" must return in our theology to the place that God's patience has given it in history. The "world" is neither all nature nor all humanity nor all "culture"; it is structured unbelief, rebellion taking with it a fragment of what should have been the order of the kingdom. It is not just an "attitude," as is supposed by the shallow interiorization of attempts to locate "worldliness'" in the mind alone. Nor is it to be shallowly exteriorized and equated with certain catalogued and forbidden leisure-time occupations. There are acts and institutions which are by their nature—and not solely by an accident of context or motivation—denials of faith in Christ.

The problem is also wrongly located when H. Richard Niebuhr sets up over against Christ a quantity named "culture" which one may then attempt to relate to Christ in a number of possible ways. In spite of the effectiveness of this scheme as a tool for classification and teaching, in spite of the erudition and sympathetic understanding with which Niebuhr deals with the various possibilities, and in spite of the literary qualities which have won the book its broad circulation, it must be recognized that his fundamental Christ/culture polarity, and typology of possible ethical standards which he builds upon it, are at bottom unfair to history and unfruitful for ethics. The reason for this is the assumption that culture "as such," i.e., as distinct from Christ, is a tangible reality patient of being related consistently to "Christ" in one of the five typical ways. This is to attribute to the world that intrinsic ontological dignity which neither the New Testament nor history allows it to claim. We must affirm the reality of the world, but not by ascribing to it the right to the place it usurps.

The awareness of the visible reality of the world leads to two scandalous conclusions. The first is that Christian ethics is for Christians. Since Augustine this has been denied; the first criterion for an ethical ideal for laymen is its generalizability. From Kant's rigorous philosophical formulation of this criterion, to the lay application in questions like, "What would happen if we were all pacifists like you?" the presupposition is universal that the right will have to apply as a simple, performable possibility for a whole society. Thus, the choice is between demanding of everyone a level of obedience and selflessness which only faith and forgiveness make meaningful (the puritan alternative) and lowering the requirements for everyone to the level where faith and forgiveness will not be needed (the medieval alternative). This dilemma is not part of the historical situation; it is an artificial construction springing from a failure to recognize the reality of the world.

The second scandalous conclusion is that there may well be certain functions in a given society which that society in its unbelief considers necessary, and which the unbelief renders in fact necessary, in which Christians will not be called to participate. This was self-evident in the early

Christian view of the state; that it had to be rejected later becomes less and less self-evident the longer we live and learn.

This view of the church commends itself exegetically and theologically. Contrary to the opposing view, it refuses to accept pragmatic grounds for deciding how Christians should relate themselves to the world. And yet after saying this we observe that this Biblical approach is in fact the most effective. The moral renewal of England in the eighteenth century was the fruit not of the Anglican establishment but of the Wesleyan revival. The Christianization of Germanic Europe in the Middle Ages was not achieved by the state church structure, with an incompetent priest in every village and an incontinent Christian on every throne, but by the orders, with the voluntaristic base, the demanding discipline, the mobility, and the selectivity as to tasks which characterize the free-church pattern. What moral tone there is in today's Germany is due not to the state-allied church and the church-allied political parties, but to the bootleg Bruderschaften of the Barmen confession.

This makes it clear that the current vogue of the phrase "responsible society" in ecumenical circles is a most irresponsible use of terms. Even if we let pass the intentional ambiguity which makes society both the subject and the object of the responsibility, and the further confusion caused by the hypostatizing of "society," there remains a fundamental misdefinition, furthered by a misreading of socio-ethical history. It continues to work with the Constantinian formulation of the problem, as if the alternatives were "responsibility" and "withdrawal." The body of thought being disseminated under this slogan is a translation into modern terms of the two ancient axioms: that the most effective way for the church to be responsible for society is for her to lose her visible specificity while leavening the lump; and that each vocation bears in itself adequately knowable inherent norms. Thus, we are invited to repeat the mistake of the Reformation, and that just at the time when the younger churches, themselves in an essentially pre-Constantinian position, need to be helped to think in other terms than those of the *Corpus Christianum* framework which has already dechristianized Europe.

Christ's victory over the world is to be dated not AD 311 or 313 but AD 29 or 30. That church will partake most truly of his triumph which follows him most faithfully in that warfare whose weapons are not carnal but mighty. She will be most effective when she abandons effectiveness and intelligence in favor of the foolish weakness of the cross in which are the wisdom and the power of God. She will be most deeply and lastingly responsible for those in the valley of the shadow if she is the city set on the hill. The true church is the free church.

How then do we face de-Constantinization? If we meet it as just another turn of the inscrutable screw of providence, just one more chance to state the Constantinian position in new terms, then the judgment which has already begun will sweep us along in the collapse of the culture for which we boast that we are responsible. But if we have an ear to hear what the Spirit says to the churches; if we let ourselves be led out of the inferiority complex which the theologies of the Reformation have thus far imposed on free church thought; if we discover as brethren in a common cause the catacomb churches of East Germany and the Bruderschaften of East Germany; if we puncture the "American dream" and discover that even in the land of the God-trusting post office and the Bible-believing chaplaincy we are in the same essentially missionary situation, the same minority status as the church in Ceylon or Colombia; if we believe that the free church, and not the free world, is the primary bearer of God's banner, the fullness of him who fills all in all; if we face de-Constantinization not as just another dirty trick of destiny but as the overdue providential unveiling of a pernicious error, then it may be given to us, even in the twentieth century, to be the church. For what more could we ask?

—— Part II ——
On Political Ideologies
Articles from CONCERN 10 (1961)

5

Christian Thought in the Age of the Cold War

Jan M. Lochmann

The Unconditional Yea! of the Gospel

> *The gospel is the heralding of God's action for the world, to save and to summon. God's action expresses the unequivocal and unconditional Yes! of his grace, which saves and lays claim on the whole man.*

In the incarnation, crucifixion, and resurrection of Jesus Christ God takes sides with the world, takes its guilt upon himself, and thereby pronounces his gracious Yea! to the world. This divine Yea is not dependent on any human prerequisites; it is unconditional and unlimited. It embraces all peoples and races, recognizing no political, social, religious, or cultural differences. It reaches man in the depths of his common humanity as a gift of grace, seeking man's life and welfare. Even the "No" of God's commands and judgments must, in the light of the gospel, be properly grasped as an expression of his positive love for man.

The gospel which announces this Yes of God in Jesus Christ at the same time commits those who confess it to discipleship and thereby to unconditional self-abandon and love toward men. Faith makes it impossible for a confessing Christian to deal with his fellowman without taking into account Christ who died for him. It is therefore impossible for the Christian to deal with him hatefully, or to harm him or his honor.

PART II: ON POLITICAL IDEOLOGIES

> *Every attempt to circumscribe the Gospel results in a distortion of doctrine and of the Church, through which either the consolation or the command of God's Grace is curtailed.*

In the history of doctrine and of the church we can follow these efforts to circumscribe the unconditional character of God's Yes. Again and again Christendom lacked the courageous faith which dares to lean only on the grace of God. The circumcision controversy in the churches of the apostle Paul provides an early and graphic example. Whenever the gospel is bound to a church, a race, a people, a culture, a civilization, or an ideology, this means a curtailment of the gospel and the enslavement of Christian faith. Such a curtailment occurs in one of two basic forms; as a curtailment of the promise of the gospel (*Zuspruch*) or of its claim (*Anspruch*).

The Curtailment of the Promise of the Gospel

> *The absolute self-giving of God to men is curtailed in the church when the church usurps the cause of Christ as her own, claims God's authority as her own, and feels called to dominate rather than to serve.*

It is an evident temptation for the church to take the gospel into her own hands, to regard the *beneficia Christi* as her monopoly and to limit the free grace of God to her own channels and to the recipients she chooses. Already in the earliest centuries we can observe this misunderstanding of the church. This temptation led to Rome, i.e., to that form of the church which requisitions the salvation of mankind for herself, with the practical result that she claims divine authority for the intellectual, cultural, and social mores and institutions which she has developed. As if not the Lord Jesus Christ, but his earthly vicars were sitting at the Right Hand of God! As if his disciples should take a path different from his own, not giving themselves in unhesitating service and devotion to the world, but rather seeking guardianship and dominion over it. Thanks to the word of the prophets and apostles, the Reformation uncovered this error of Romanism. Yet the romanistic temptation remained and often threatened the church of the Reformation (and her dignitaries!). After World War II, did not the definitely romanist idea of a "Christian political party" (with all it involves, including the mentality of the crusade) find sympathy in Protestant circles? Therefore, we must clearly affirm: the attempt to take the cause of Christ in one's own hands, for oneself and against others, leads to the curtailment and the abuse of the gospel.

> *The power of the resurrection and the ascension of Christ are curtailed if the preservation of former ecclesiastical institutions under changed social conditions is considered as the theologically legitimate purpose of the church.*

Not only when she falls prey to the temptations of power politics does the church curtail the gospel; she does so already when she clings to the traditional forms and patterns of ecclesiastical life. Church organizations are historical phenomena. As such they always—and especially today, in the revolutions of technical civilization—encounter new socio-political and cultural situations. These changes exert a strong influence on the life of the church. Yet it is theologically false to view them with a prior hostility in an effort to maintain traditional forms. The task of the church in the world is not to survive at any price, but to serve the world by proclaiming and following the will of God. Where this occurs as it should, the church will form new patterns of common life more appropriate to the new conditions. Jesus Christ's Lordship is not bound to church institutions; rather, he rules the whole world for the sake of that pilgrim band which travels through one upset after another to meet him.

> *The gospel is legalized and its liberty curtailed when it is understood and treated as an ideology. It is drawn into the conflict of ideologies and loses its transcendent sovereignty.*

In Jesus Christ God has concerned himself with all of man. The gospel is not simply a doctrine; God's word is also his deed, the turning point not merely of religious thought but of all human existence. In its center there stands not an idea but the real man Jesus Christ. Thus, the gospel also has to do with ideologies—religious and otherwise—as component elements of human existence, but does not lose itself in them, is not identified with them but rather transcends them. This transcendence is misapprehended and denied when it is confused with an ideology, and when theology is handled apologetically or aggressively as one doctrine over against other doctrines. Not only is the free word of the living God which is above all human wisdom thereby dragged down to the all too human level of ideological controversy; even worse, its real intention is thereby misunderstood. Jesus Christ, who is the Salvation of the whole of man, is reduced to an element of human understanding; the Lord and Savior is made a partisan in an ideological debate.

> *The reality of the incarnation is misapprehended in its full significance and idealistically distorted when a battle line is drawn between the gospel and materialistic atheism. Genuine encounter with, and witness to, the materialistic neighbor is thereby threatened.*

Especially when she encounters materialistic atheism is the church tempted to draw a false battle line. She seeks to resist its rejection of all religions as idealism by allying herself with idealistic polemics and apologetics. As if the cause of Christ and the work of the Holy Spirit were identical with idealism in general, as if the gospel were really struck by the attack against idealistic polemics and apologetics. As if the cause of Christ and it is a misunderstanding of the gospel. It wrongly conceives the reality of the incarnation, which is the very center of the Christian message, God's giving himself to the real world—both "spirit" and "matter." Thus, the atheistic critique of religion demonstrates that it has not grasped and therefore not refuted the essence of the gospel. Yet, the church has furthered this misunderstanding when she has encountered atheism in the wrong way, namely as an ally of idealism. Thus, the real conflict between the word of God and all ideologies has become an opposition between ideologies. The church's testimony to the atheist is rendered difficult, if not impossible. Only when the Christian rejection of materialism is the result not of a prior idealistic prejudice, but of a deep grasp of the valid kernel of materialism's concern (its taking the real world and the material needs of man seriously, which biblical thought understands), is it genuine and believable. Only when the church's No to atheism rings out not as systematic opposition but as a testimony of Christian solidarity with even the godless brother, for whom Christ died and rose, will the false barrier be broken through and the way opened to genuine encounter and testimony to the atheist.

> *The gospel is legalized when it is bound to a particular confessional expression or a peculiar terminology, where beside the free word of God a particular doctrinal tradition is set up as normative, where a church mistakes her understanding of the truth for possession of truth.*

The gospel is also ideologized when the church conceives it as a fixed doctrinal system. This is the danger of every confessionalism. Valid theology will always hearken gratefully to the voice of the fathers, as a sign of the communion which binds Christians across the divisions of time as well as of space. But such communion is a gift of the Holy Spirit, and where he breathes, there is freedom, not the bondage to the dead letter. This is what confessionalism misunderstands. The letter of the fathers' witness is taken not in spiritual seriousness, but in "dead earnest." The truth of the living Lord Jesus Christ—who is ever anew his own best witness—is fixed, and thereby subjected to the church and her teachers, to be used in opposition to others.

The Curtailment of the Claim of the Gospel

> *In Jesus Christ God enters into the whole depth and breadth of human existence. In all the depth and breadth of his life man is confronted with Jesus Christ and summoned to discipleship.*

The consolation, peace, and salvation of the Christian life is that nothing human is indifferent or foreign to the concern of God in Jesus Christ: "God is on our side!" But this fact that to God in Jesus Christ nothing is indifferent or foreign is at the same time an obligation, a demand, a summons to discipleship: we are on God's side! The demand is as unconditional as was the promise. There are no levels and spheres of life, where man labors and suffers as an individual or in society, in which the call to discipleship might be suspended. The gospel is the power and light for all of life.

> *The gospel is the power and light for all human existence. It is distorted wherever it is conceived and lived only "religiously," i.e., as dealing with transcendence and with inwardness, having nothing to do with "worldly concerns."*

The gospel is the end of religion as man's effort piously to lay hold of God by his own effort. Nonetheless, religion has through the centuries remained the great temptation of the church. The enfleshed word was religiously "stylized." God the Center of all real life became deity in general; his requisitioning of the truly human in all its forms became a liturgical-cultic manner of life; Christ's Lordship over the universe became his rule over "my soul." Undeniably many flowers of deep piety have been cultivated in the church's history, from ancient and medieval mysticism to recent pietism. With it there has been—especially in pietism—much genuinely loving service. Nevertheless, cultivated inwardness (whether cultic and liturgical, mystical and quietist, pietistic, or academically theological in form) is, if made the major thrust of the Christian life, a distortion of the gospel through its turning away from the world especially from the realm of public responsibility; a curtailment of the gospel's relevance, a spirit of resignation which contrasts with the creative spirit of faith, love, and hope. The church which in her discipleship sees herself responsible for all humanity, will recognize—especially among the menaces of the atomic age—the temptation to a religious distortion of the gospel.

> The gospel is the power and light of all human existence. It is perniciously curtailed when the Christian life is understood within a dualism such that only certain realms may be measured. and patterned by the gospel, and in others the word of Jesus is consciously considered not to be binding or not relevant.

The radical claim of Jesus Christ, his deepening and bursting of all traditional commandments especially in the Sermon on the Mount is so unheard of that its application to problems within this fallen world has been understood, also within the churches, as fanaticism. It is true enough that a too direct, legalistically imitative application of Jesus's words might be a fanatical misinterpretation. Here lies the valid thrust of the *Zwei-Reiche* (two-kingdom) doctrine, which, however, was understood dualistically. The gospel is a spiritual word, valid for the realms of faith and the church; civil life in this unredeemed world is another realm, in which not the gospel but law, not the word of Jesus but words of our minds are determining. In spite of its justified point of departure this dualistic doctrine—especially in its later forms—is biblically untenable. The gospel is evacuated too globally from important areas of life, such as, traditionally, from that of economic and political life. This has meant that for all practical purposes the Lordship of Christ was suspended in wide areas of life, which were then abandoned to reason—or, as experience shows, to unreason and the blind will to power. This we must combat, not alone in its consequences, but in its political rootage. Jesus Christ is relevant even for politics. His unconditional self-giving to men shines into even the most confused problems of political and social life, not as human law but as gospel; as a summons to an unconditional will to peace with the neighbor.

The Curtailment of the Gospel as the Point of Entry for Cold War into the Church

> Cold War is an attempt to coerce the adversary with any means, even with the threat of hot war. In the church, Cold War is the effort to libel and label the adversary as an enemy of God and to excommunicate him.

We are living in the age of the Cold War. In the atomic age an open "hot" war has become politically unusable. There are no political purposes which could be attained after the general atomic annihilation which hot war today means. In such a situation a Cold War is launched, to intimidate, weaken and to push back the opponent with ideological, psychological, and economic pressure. On all sides the church is tempted as well to let herself be harnessed to the Cold War wagon. Especially where one group of peoples is admittedly guided by a materialistic ideology, efforts are made from the other side to dress up economic and political interests with religious adjectives and to identify them with Christian civilization or with Christianity itself. This provides the most poisonous of Cold War weapons, for the political adversary is labelled as an enemy of God and of the truth, as "Godless" and "murderer of souls," with whom no more communication is possible, good only to be cast out. Cold War in the church supplies the poison for the political Cold War.

> *The gospel of the unconditionally reconciling love of God for men is the spirit and the power of peace, utterly incompatible with the spirit of the Cold War. Cold War can prosper in the church only when the gospel is curtailed.*

Cold War is basically . . . war! Without shooting, one learns to consider the adversary as someone who really should be shot at, whom one at least should intimidate, weaken, and drive back. Thus, the spirit of war is ever-present, the Spirit of him who is "a murderer from the beginning" (John 8:44), i.e., a killer before the act of killing. This spirit is diametrically opposed to the spirit of Jesus, who by his death and resurrection completely vanquished the satanic spirit of war—of Cold War between God and man and Cold War between men. His authoritative Easter proclamation was simply the word "peace." Thus, is Cold War in the church actually a contradiction in terms, if by church we mean the ecclesia of Jesus Christ. Only when the church and her theology fall into unbelief, i.e., when in meeting concrete problems she overlooks the gospel of Jesus and thinks and lives in another spirit, can she be recruited consciously or unconsciously for the Cold War. Only a curtailed, misunderstood, and misused gospel can forge the weapons of Cold War. Let us in summary again attempt to characterize the two basic types of this curtailment.

> *In the legalistic curtailment of its promise the gospel is understood as the possession of truth, self-righteously conceived as in opposition to others. The Cold War spirit is thereby directly or indirectly furthered.*

The common denominator of all these most varied forms of curtailment of the promise of the gospel is legalism. The free and unlimited grace and truth of God are relegated to fixed channels, bound more or less exclusively to a certain historical church, institution, ideology, or creed. Thus, the gospel loses its sovereignty and is subjected to law. Since such law is created and defined by men, this means the gospel is in effect in men's hands. The churchman and theologian think of himself—consciously or not—as a truth-possessor. But the spirit of the legalistic truth-possessor is one of self-justification. He whom this spirit drives is incapable of veritable communication with a neighbor of differing conviction; from the outset he is right, the other wrong. This is the root of the churches' Cold War; it is "the Christianly disguised war between truth-possessors justifying themselves by their possession of truth" (Heinrich Vogel). A pernicious irreconcilableness stokes the fires of war, the crusaders are provided with a good conscience and the walls are built ever higher; the Cold War in the churches provokes and reinforces the general Cold War.

> *In the dualist limitation of its claim, the gospel is dismissed from certain realms of Christian responsibility. The forces of Cold War are thus tolerated or even religiously justified in the name of "Christian Realism."*

Every dualistic conception of the gospel—e.g., the quietistic-pietistic or the extreme *Zwei-Reiche* doctrine—actually eliminates the relevance of the word of Christ from broad realms of human experience. The vacuum thus created is to be filled by reasonable human judgment. But church history teaches otherwise: if the claim of the gospel is limited or suspended, then what steps into the breach is man's unbridled will to power. Under the cover of the quietists or the two-kingdom dualists political cynics come to power. This is not accidental; they find a bridgehead in such (subjectively very pious and earnest) doctrine. "The whole world lieth in the evil one," "all men are guilty," "There is none that doeth good, no, not one"—these true biblical pronouncements are deeply understood by the dualist, but then they are abstractly generalized and thereby misinterpreted and extended into false political conclusions, as if only "realistic" power politics were fitting to fallen human nature. We know the practical results of this position;

its fatal tolerance, yea even reactionary advocacy of the powerful. We recognize these results as well in contemporary "atomic theology," which uses abundantly this ideology. The powers of the Cold War thrive in the shadow of dualism. But it is also just at this point that we can see strikingly how untenable such thought is before the gospel; to draw even atomic mass murder and suicide within the circle of theologically justifiable possibilities completely shatters the framework of evangelical thought (if "evangelical" is to have any meaning as testifying to a relationship to the gospel). This ultimate consequence unmasks dualism as a denial of the faith.

Banning Cold War from the Church

> *The Cold War is overcome in the church when she dares to live the unabridged gospel in spite of all temptation, permitting herself to be overcome by nothing other than the peace of Jesus Christ. In faithfulness to this gospel the Christian will find the way opening to reasonable political service to men in our day.*

The "one thing needed" in evangelicalism has always been to live from the whole gospel. It has always been the basic task of evangelical theology to ward off every distortion of the gospel in the church. But seldom has the immediate practical relevance of this task—all the way into the political realm—been as openly visible as it is today. In the age of the atomic menace, it is certainly one of the most urgent tasks of politics to eliminate the Cold War with its constantly latent danger of total annihilation. The faithful church must accept this task as her own, especially by doing everything possible to set her own house in order, purging from the church the points of affinity with Cold War thought and thereby contributing to healing and reconciliation in the poisoned atmosphere of world politics. She can do so, for she has been entrusted with the gospel, the inexhaustible and radical power of reconciliation and peace. There is no other power of this depth, just as there is no other inexhaustible and radical devotion to Man than that of Jesus Christ. This is no mere formal theological statement or rhetorical exaggeration. Today discipleship is seen as practically and politically realistic and reasonable, yea as perhaps the only practicable way of Christian orientation. What hitherto sounded realistic ("realist power politics") is today sterile and utopian. What hitherto seemed utopian (the radical path of peace and reconciliation in the spirit of the Sermon on the Mount) has become realistic. Therefore, is it so eminently important that the church not hide her light under a bushel but undaunted stand by the whole gospel. This is important not only for her own sake but for the world. Our serving the gospel of peace and reconciliation is an essential service to mankind. That we might again know this, that we might experience the growing relevance of this service even to the political realm, is for our theological and churchly work a gift full of promise. A great gift and a great obligation!

6

Christians and Marxists

Albert Gaillard

A fundamental ambiguity threatens when we speak of Christians and Communists as if we were dealing with two positions which are spiritually comparable. Christianity is above all a faith; Marxism refuses to be considered as a faith, commending itself as a rigorously scientific procedure: first, a rational explanation of the contradictions of history, and then a dialectically conceived action to bring in the just society.

It is therefore always possible to define the Communist by his adhesion to Marxist-Leninist doctrine (as unceasingly reoriented in light of the historical conjuncture) or by his belonging to the Party. It is never possible to define the Christian in the same manner; he who adheres to the doctrine of the church or registers as a member is not necessarily Christian. This is the problem of Christian authenticity: without a living faith which ties one to Jesus Christ and which changes one's way of life, there is neither Christian nor Christianity. There is thus a fundamental misunderstanding, more and more deeply built into our language, when we speak in the same way of Christians and of Communists. There is no civilization or state or party that is specifically Christian; whereas there are Communist states and parties and a Communist civilization.

This ambiguity is therefore built-in whenever we undertake to oppose or compare the behavior of Christians and that of Communists or to evaluate the possibility, the conditions, and the nature of relations between Christians and Communists.

The ambiguity is still greater—or at least it is maintained—by the contradictory image of Christianity which is offered by Roman Catholicism.

We must not forget that many are acquainted with Christianity only through Catholicism, i.e., through a church committed for sixteen centuries to "Constantinianism," to the point that it appears not only as a state with its ambassadors (the apostolic *nuncios* and treaties of alliance [concordats]), but also as a supra-national power determining openly or secretly the policies of other states; consider for example the role played in Western Europe by the Catholic parties or by the mysterious allegiance of important statesmen to the secular order *Opus Dei*.

I may presuppose a general awareness of Marxism's vision of history and doctrine of man. Apparently, it is a simple matter. Christians live in the knowledge that Jesus Christ is the Lord of their own life and of all history. The appearance of Christ is for them the decisive event of history. Their hope is altogether dependent upon Christ, his resurrection, and his kingdom. In Christ, human history is potentially summed-up; economic or social upsets can henceforth change nothing.

For the Communist, the perspective is quite different. True, there is a rigorous historical determinism which leaves no more to change than does the Christian view. Still the gamble has not yet been won, for man in his fullness does not yet exist, has not been realized. Man is in the process of creating himself, via the evolution of a society in conflict with nature and constantly hindered by its own internal contradictions. Man is still becoming. What he shall be is just barely discernable amidst all the inhumanity which persists. Social and economic relationships will condition what he becomes.

But in reality, things are not so simple. For Communism nourishes an extreme optimism with regard to history, and this implies in turn a profound confidence in man's "becoming." We should attempt to understand Communists from the perspective of this confidence rather than beginning simply with "historical materialism."

Of course, Communists hold economic factors to be primordial, and it is the development of the means of production which explains for them all human history and its conflicts. But it certainly would be unfair to relegate Marxism to what Marx himself called, in a pejorative tone, "vulgar materialism." Already in 1890, Engles had carefully underlined, "Marx and I are perhaps to blame for our disciples' having sometimes insisted too much on the economic factors. We were obliged to insist on their fundamental importance, because our adversaries denied them; we did not always have the time or the occasion to do justice to the other factors." This honest admission finds an effort in Mao Tse-tung: "We recognize that in the course of historical development the material determines the spiritual and social reality determines the social conscience, but we recognize at the same time—and must do-so—the reciprocal action of the spiritual on the material, of social conscience on social reality, of the superstructure on the economic base. In so doing we do not contradict materialism; in refuting mechanical materialism we defend dialectical materialism."[1] And the French Marxist Garaudy declares in a much-noticed work, "Materialism implies a practical combat against everything which crushes and degrades man; the struggle for material welfare conditions, the struggle for other values, including the spiritual. . . . His alienation once overcome, Man will find fulfilment. The needs he will satisfy will no longer be the biological needs which hounded him in the beginning, namely hunger and the revolt against suffering, but the needs of every dimension of human life." Marxist anthropology is thus more refined than one might suppose.

If from the doctrinal level we move to that of daily existence, it is possible to observe—at least in France—a certain disquiet quiet concerning the official optimism of the Party toward history and its confidence in man. An authentic self-criticism, still subject to Party supervision, is visible among Communist intellectuals whose lucidity, honesty, and courage are equally admirable. The recent *Basic Criticism* of Jean Baby, typical in this respect, concludes, "The tragedy of the Communist Party is that it is obsessed by the need to justify everything it has ever done. The scarecrow of 'revisionism' is brandished as if this were the only danger, whereas we should first combat sectarianism, arid dogmatism, and the refusal to recognize one's faults-which are the best fuel for revisionism." Speaking of Communism's relationships with intellectuals, which he notes are deteriorating, Baby declares, "Primarily the Party used the names of well-known persons to give more weight to its demonstrations; it was very unconcerned to discuss with them, in the spirit of the free conversation, the problems with which they were preoccupied. When thorny questions arose, the Party replaced free discussion, to which intellectuals are necessarily devoted, with a narrow dogmatism and a disrespectful brutality which wounded them deeply. The classic example of the Affaire Lysenko is still in every one's minds."

This is not the expression of a simple polemist. Numerous personal contacts, maintained for years, with Communist intellectuals, have convinced me that many of them are deeply troubled, as became visible for the first

---

1. Tse-tung, "On Contradiction," 336.

time in 1956–57 at the occasion of the Hungary crisis. This is not so much a hesitation in the face of violence when it reveals its incapacity to achieve justice; such a reaction would remain theoretical. The reason is rather the discovery of a certain inhumanity in the practical outworking of revolution, calling forth a protest in favor of man. It is a moving experience to encounter such concrete humanistic concern precisely among Communists.

Here we must place a very important remark concerning the Christian approach. It is easy to identify persons with the philosophical or political system which they confess. But this identification is never totally possible, even among Communists. Christians should be lucid enough to discern this. But especially they should be capable to avoid aggressive consistency which would remove all further possibility of human contact and thereby of testimony.

This is not self-evident. For a certain number of Christians (and churches) their faith implies a systematic anti-Communism which can go, if necessary, as far as the Crusade. It is strange to say the least, that Christians, proclaiming themselves resolutely anti-Marxist, thus adapt the Marxist vision of history, accepting so materialistic a view of its course that they wish to assure the triumph of their Christianity by the sword. It seems to me to be difficult to reconcile the reality of the Lordship of Jesus Christ and an eschatological hope with the use of such means.

But there is a still more subtle temptation; that of the Christian "ghetto" within which one barricades oneself to avoid dangerous contacts. The essential need of contemporary humanity is precisely for encounter, communication, dialogue. To avoid this is not a mistake but a sin. Not only does one thus shut oneself in within his sheltered ghetto; the others are at the same time shut out, in what we denounce as their false doctrine, and this is immeasurably more serious because it may mean closing to them the door to the kingdom of God. The Christian witness implies sincere concern for others, an unselfish openness of spirit toward them, and the absence of pharisaism and self-righteousness.

I have learned much through my personal contacts with Communists. I have discovered the seriousness of their conviction, the devotion with which they serve, the spirit of sacrifice which drives them, I have understood the authentic human concern which motivates their passion for social justice. I believe that it is a part of the Christian witness to render esteem, respect, friendship, and sympathy to such men. Furthermore, such an attitude is beginning to be expressed, timidly as yet, within official

Catholicism, marked though Rome has been by an anti-Marxism in principle. In a pastoral letter of April 25, 1960, read from all the pulpits in his diocese on May 1 (Labor Day), Mgr. Lacointe, Bishop of Beauvais, Noyon, and Senlis, wrote as follows of the daily contact between Catholic and Communist working-men within the factory: "Christian workers will meet men and women more or less under Marxist influence, who however retain a certain desire for liberty, a distaste for dictatorship, and even a certain love for Christ. Shall Christians turn their backs to this whole world, thinking thus to be in security? It would be contrary to the order of Christ." Edmond Michelet, Catholic Minister in the Fifth Republic, did not hesitate to say to a congress of Catholic intellectuals, "Communism may be 'intrinsically perverse'; Communists are not, if only because they are men. . . . When we are honored to share without solicitation, the confidences of some Communists, we are sometimes surprised to discover an echo of humane concern of utter authenticity."

But we must go beyond this elementary evidence of humane benevolence. Christians must further recognize what is valid in Communism, taking it seriously instead of suspecting it, ready to learn from it. We cannot take refuge in a kind of Manichean myth which would consider everything Marxist as belonging to the kingdom of darkness.

One of the most serious reproaches addressed by Communists to churches and Christians is that of paying no attention to unjust social structures, caring only for man's spiritual salvation. This reproach we must admit is well-founded.

Every time Christians tolerate social injustice, every time they permit men's subjection and alienation by the power of money, their indifference to the economic and social context is a denial of the Lordship of Christ and a betrayal of his gospel. The church can then maintain an apparent orthodoxy, but her most correct doctrinal phrases have been emptied of their "prophetic" content, i.e., of the Lord's living word to the world. Thus when after the "Cleveland declaration" J. Howard Pew, former chairman of a laymen's committee of the Presbyterian Church (and of the Sun Oil Company), "warns his church that wealthy men would continue to withhold their contributions from the corporate church until she stops speaking on social issues such as the civic rights of negroes and the demands of labor," he is a more redoubtable adversary of the Lordship of Christ than M. Khrushchev.

Then we must draw the positive lessons of this kind of awareness. Though Communists are wrong, excessively optimistic, when they think that the coming of a just society will suffice to change man and make him righteous, they are nonetheless right in insisting indefatigably on the urgency of establishing a just social order—against the will, obviously, of those who benefit from injustice—in order to safeguard man, "the most precious capital."

Doubtless Christians will have to begin to listen humbly to this message which is found throughout the Bible, but which they have let themselves be deprived of through failing to translate it into today's social context. We suffer the cruel lack of a Christian social ethic. Retracing naively the Biblical ethic will not do; it would be ridiculous to try to apply to modern society the social laws of Deuteronomy, remarkable as they were in their time. Yet it is urgent that we ask what conception of man and of his social relations they implied, especially as concerns property. The needed expenditure of imagination and ethical invention to attain worldwide dimensions is great. The individual ethics with which we have been satisfied will not reach. The greatest crimes against man are committed not by individuals but by groups (classes, nations, races) against groups. To combat the hunger which every year kills millions we must radically modify the system of economic privilege which places four-fifths of the world's wealth in the hands of one-third of the people. To combat illiteracy or the slum we must decide whether to finance war or construction and education. It is self-evident that this cannot be done without seriously modifying economic liberalism. Even though the church has no expert competence in political economics, she can and must discern clearly that liberty is not genuine when it is a selfish privilege which a few withhold from others.

Thus, Christians must listen to Communists; let us do it humbly, for we have a lag of a century—or fifteen—to make up!

Beginning with such an attitude, dialogue with Communists can be fruitful. I noted earlier that in the thought of the best theorists of Marxism—beginning with Marx and Engels themselves—one can find an embryonic awareness of the role of spiritual values. The brittleness of Christians, their suspicious prejudice, their defensive reflexes will never help Communists to develop further this beginning. On the contrary; such an attitude calls forth a heightened mistrust of spiritual values, suspect of serving as the alibi of an easy conscience and a veritable opium for the victims of the capitalist economy. Thus, we fall into the vicious circle of reciprocal accusations. In such a way there can be no evangelization of the Communist world. By rejecting unexamined the stray fragments of truth which Marxism treasures—however mixed with dross—Christians close doors for the gospel. Emanuel Mounier saw clearly:

> Communism and Christianity are bound to one another like Jacob and the angel, in a severity and a fraternity of combat which is immeasurably more weighty than the power that is at stake. It would be too easy to make Communism the Antichrist. It contains anti-Christian elements, as does the "Christian world" itself; but it contains as well, and this is its mysterious mission, a share of the Kingdom of God. What most polemics between the two fail to realize is that Christians and Communists, even when engaged in a pitched battle, keep a secret relationship which neither can repudiate. Whence comes the constant embarrassment of the combatants.

Permit me to share a personal experience which I have repeated many times in recent years in dialogues with Communists. Every time I have been thus attentive to their demands for justice embodied in a socialist structure, I have led them to admit in their turn the necessity for a deep change in human nature going beyond the changes caused by the new economic and social structure. Christians have too long neglected or underestimated the importance of such structures, and the power with which economic and social realities form human beings. The consequences of the technical revolution of the last quarter-century will force Christians to recognize their misapprehension and to change their behavior. This price they must pay for Marxists to cease to consider them as "idealists," chasers after the nonexistent, with no impact on the movement of history, unless it be to slow it by their conservatism.

In return, when Christians have become attentive to the importance of these factors in molding men, and recognize their past error of judgment, it is very rare that they do not obtain rapidly an understanding and sometimes moving attention to the specific element of their own Christian witness, namely the necessity that human mentality be transformed far more thoroughly, to enable men to love justice, love truth, and love liberty for others. In the face of frustrations of his own hopes, the Marxist can be led to see that the revolution of structures can never attain the full human value it seeks, except in and through a spiritual revolution which changes man himself.

I am more and more convinced that in the present context—in the Christian church and in Marxist socialism, each in its present form—there exists a certain provisional complementarity. Instead of barricading ourselves within our doctrinal pride and our anathemas we must learn from one another in fruitful dialogue.

There remain the official atheism and the dialectical materialism of Communism, which can be held up as an insurmountable obstacle to real encounter. For the interlocuters need at least a minimum of common vocabulary! The objection is serious, at least theoretically.

But alas, is there not among Christians a practical atheism which behaves in the world as if they were not living under the Lordship of Christ, as if their doctrine were only a Sunday luxury (Marx would say "superstructure") without connection to their daily life and without influence upon their social relationships? Is there not among Christians a practical materialism which consists in settling down as comfortably as possible in the world which will pass away, as if the kingdom of God were never coming?

The Communists will not fail to throw up to us this striking inconsistency and to draw therefrom, by contrast, a justification of the economic and social efficacy of Marxism. Most often they are sincere in their self-righteous view of Christianity, and the Christians are at fault. Today more than a century ago, we can observe what Marx called Christianity's "loss of function."

As a matter of fact, since the fifth century Christendom no longer lives in the hope of the kingdom of God, but in the eagerness to acquire jealously a place in the middle of this world, with all the secret and official compromises that this involves. There are signs, every day more numerous and more clear, that we are reaching the end of this "Constantinian" era. The decisive influence of Marxism on more than half of humanity in 1960 should lead the churches to carry through rapidly their "political" purge. The Christian must demonstrate daringly that he has bet on the Lordship of Jesus Christ and votes for a joyful acceleration of history rather than a fearful conservatism clinging to the past.

In the Hellenistic world the apostle Paul confronted a situation no less ambiguous and difficult. The world was overflowing with gods and idols, and with skeptics as well. The risk was great when the ambassador of Christ got mixed up with all the philosophers and rhetors, all those pagans. What did the apostle do? "Free from all, I made myself the slave of all, in order to win as many as possible; Jew with the Jew, subject to the

Law with those who are subject to the Law, Law-less with the Law-less, I made myself all things to all men in order at any cost to save some" (1 Cor 9:19–22). Who can fail to see that the ardent flame which burned within the apostle had nothing to do with opportunism or imprudence? "I made it my boast to preach the Gospel where the name of Christ had never been spoken" (Rom 15:20). Thus, he cared neither for the ideologies nor for the systems in which they were involved; he looked at men, could see only men, miserable creatures but loved and saved by Jesus Christ.

Can we pierce through the incrustations of nineteen centuries? In the midst of our atomic age, as socialism rises the challenger, will we be able to stop being the hostages of Right or Left and become again genuine ambassadors of the Lord Jesus Christ, with the credentials of the Sermon on the Mount, the language of divine mercy, and the unmasked visage of brotherly love?

7

Where Are the Firemen?

Katharina van Drimmelen

Communism, a Challenge to Christianity

In certain parts of the world it seems hardly possible to speak about Communism in an unemotional way. Most people are convinced that they are against Communism, but often this is merely an emotional response.

Much of this, in my opinion, is the background of the John Birch Society and, similarly, of films like Operation Abolition. They do more harm than good, creating feelings without giving real information about the facts. Perhaps few people realize that the emotional side of the Cold War, in which we are involved whether we like it or not, is one of the strongest weapons in the very hands of Communism. President Kennedy must have had this in mind, when he spoke his courageous words: "We won't fear to negotiate, but we won't negotiate our fear."

There is a different way however, to consider Communism, which I would like to call knowing and facing the facts. And then, in a most realistic way, confronting them with Christianity.

Communism Has To Be Taken Seriously

In our time there is no use hiding ourselves from the realistic fact that Communism, both its ideology and its political consequences, has a great influence in the entire world. The Russian Revolution, early this century, has set a nation on fire and this has been spreading around ever since, with, as it seems, too few firemen present to extinguish it. This is a serious fact, which can be ignored just as little as a real fire. Both in Russia and in the Satellite States behind the Iron Curtain, as well as in China—though Red China's attitude is to be recognized as different from Communism in Russia itself—and in the younger nations in the near and far East, Communism is powerful and it has made up its mind as to the rest of the world. We cannot be but very realistic about this. Not rebellion and riots as such are to be identified with Communism. They are to be considered as the birth pains of a new ideology, a fact, repeated in history. The only way to face Communism of today is to study it, wanting to know; without becoming emotional for the sake of mere ignorance.

It is impossible to extinguish any fire, until one has discovered the origin of it, and without capable men to do so. Communism has to be faced and studied, rather than to be feared beyond reason. Some of the characteristics, although known to many, ought to be remembered by all those, who won't negotiate their fear.

Communism Is an Atheism

This is one of the basic facts which will keep Christians from identifying themselves with Communism. According to the Darwinist theory of evolution, Communism teaches that man will be able to develop himself without any limitation, to a state of increasing perfection. Skill derived from science, the right materials, labor, and production, are the factors which will constitute and improve the life of men and will meet all his needs. There is no concept of God, for there is no need for one. "*Ohne Gott und Sonnenschein bringen wir die Ernte ein*" (Without God and without the sunshine, are we able to harvest.) Signs with these words have been put on the tractors in Eastern Germany during the harvest season. Part of this should be seen against the background of the Russian Orthodox Church and the role this Church played in Czarist Russia: the tremendous poverty of the majority of its rural population, without any changes in view; the close connection between the Czar and the Church, probably not only incorporated in the person of Rasputin; and people wondering whether God had any concern for the improvement of worse than bad social conditions. The church in Western Europe, particularly in the last decades of the nineteenth century, does not give a picture which is altogether different, becoming one of the origins of European Socialism.

Anything a Communistic and atheistic government in Russia would do, could only improve the poor conditions, for it simply was not possible to make them worse. This is one of the reasons why some of the old icons representing Christ were replaced in many Russian homes by a portrait of Lenin, who promised the nation more bread and supplied it.

At the same time, if we are ready to face the facts, we have to acknowledge that there are also Christians who are Communists, both in Russia and in Finland—which is a free country—and in many of the satellite states. How this is possible is difficult to understand for those who are having the luxury of being Christians in a free world, with too much money and too much food. I assume that those Christians who have committed themselves to Communism have dropped the atheistic aspect of it, agreeing on the social and political issues of Communism. Although we may not be able to agree, let us not forget that socialism in Western Europe at the turning of this century was by no means religious, and was opposed by all churches. After the first World War "Religious Socialism" has gotten a wide scope, and is now recognized by most of the churches, many a member of which may be a religious socialist.

Communism Promotes a Classless Anti-Capitalistic Society

The Manifesto by Marx-Engels, written in the middle of the last century, is interesting literature. I wish everybody who is opposed to Communism would take the trouble to read it, discovering how fascinating it is, for more than one reason. For here, we do not only find the bourgeoisie of the time attacked in a most violent way, but these very attacks could serve us now in order to criticize what has become of Communism in our time. The bourgeoisie being blamed by Marx for its classes, its free enterprise, and its capitalism, still seems to exist within the Russian Communistic State. Enlightening in this respect is Klaus Akkerman's book *The Treasure of Silent Millions*. Here, the author makes it clear how in Russia—in an equal, classless society, with its highly industrialized life—people are needed in order to control the equals. In the big plants, each ten or fifteen men earning an equal salary need someone to check the speed and the amount of their work. This man needs a higher salary himself, otherwise he would not be found willing to do this job. Ten or twenty of his colleagues again need someone supervising them, and of course for a higher salary. In this way the "functionaries" came into being, and thus new classes within the working society originated. The Stalinallee of East Berlin certainly does not house the average working-class man, as it is advertised. Everybody does not have a home from which the blue sky can be seen. In the apartment houses in the Stalinallee, the functionaries live and those who can afford it. And one wonders who the ladies are, who have time and money to spend a whole afternoon sipping coffee with cream cake in "Budapest," one of the most famous and expensive restaurants in the Stalinallee.

An entirely classless society seems difficult to be found under whatever government. Was not equality one of the aims of the French Revolution which violated gravestones in order to abolish the titles of even the dead?

Anti-capitalism, seems to be a more definite result of Communism. We see capitalism flourishing in almost every country in the Western world. Both in democratic countries like the United States, where free enterprise influences the market as well as the standard of living, and in democratic countries like England, Germany, and the Netherlands, with strong socialistic trends in their respective governments, where production and consumption are under state control. As long as money is the reward for labor, and an adequate reward, creating capital seems to be entirely justified. With the nature of peoples work, needs, and interests may vary. It is interesting to see statistics showing which percentage of the individual income is spent by various sociological groups on various things. But what if when people's needs are being satisfied with the normal and average income of the "status group" to which one belongs, they desire supersatisfaction; wanting to earn more money for the sake of status improvement? Do Christians have many valid arguments with which they can defend a capitalism of this kind? Christians are easily, too easily, at the defense of a thus created materialism, and we feel safe within it. We must realize that here is a real and serious point of criticism from the side of Communism, and we'd better question ourselves as to what our Christian attitudes in this should be.

Communism Hitting the Weak Spots of Christianity

Here again, knowing and facing the facts about Communism is of the greatest importance. Not everybody is aware of the fact—or are we, just misleading ourselves?—that Communism always seeks to meet those needs which the church has failed to meet. We saw this in Russia, before the Red Revolution, we see it nowadays in many places and in many fields. If the churches in South Africa fail to recognize the Bantu, not being willing for many and complicated reasons, to solve this problem, then Communism is going to take over, showing a more real interest in the oppressed. And who is to be blamed, if the Bantu will follow that policy which will make him free, or at least promises to do so?

Much is done in the Western world in order to meet the needs in India. Perhaps we, in America and in Europe, tend to believe that we are doing rather much. However, we would alter this view if we knew how many more students from India are invited to Moscow than to Europe or the United States. And how could we with an honest conscience defend the attacks made by Lenin in one of his essays, when he blames the Christians for not doing what they are believing and confessing in the church?

The Communist, convinced in what he believes as to the goal of his ideology—a better world for better people—will act with zeal equal to a truly religious zeal. Professor Banning from the Netherlands, in the first chapter of his remarkable book, *Communism: A Religion?* (translated into German, but not into English as far as I know),[1] makes the interesting statement, that to the Communist his ideology means the same as religion to the Christian.

The Russian author Maxim Gorky, in his book *Mother*,[2] gives a most valuable account of this. An old mother, opposed to the Communistic ideas of her son, at the time of the Russian Revolution, is impressed by his enthusiasm and that of his friends whom he brings home. After her son is taken to prison, she is seen carrying the red flag in a procession of laborers.

Are not Christians rightly to be questioned about their zeal and enthusiasm?

Communism a Challenge?

To some this thought may seem unbearable, but yet, why not face it? Christianity and the church as such, after being the rulers of Western society until the late Middle Ages, have lost their scope on the respective scenes of history ever since. Renaissance and Humanism in their time made Christianity more man-centered than ever before, and in our time, we suffer from an increasing remoteness of the churches from the real issues in the world. This, in my opinion, is both true for Europe and for

1. Banning and Bamm, *Der Kommunismus*.
2. Gorky, *Mother*.

America. If the church is alive at all, it lives its remote and isolated life with the believers, separating themselves from others. Is it not sad, that in Atlanta, Georgia, the lunch counters are desegregated by law, but that the table of our Lord is still segregated?

Denominations and sects have broken the totality of the body of Christ, and they have, with exception of the Roman Catholic Church, become one of the weaknesses of the church. As a Protestant, I believe in the Reformation and in its theology, which is different from Roman Catholic theology, but I cannot but regret the brokenness present in churches of the Reformation, probably even more in Europe than in the United States. As in the last century in Europe, when with the coming of industrialism the churches were not ready to face the needs of people involved, so in our time the same thing is happening again. Pietism, religiosity, self-complacency, meeting with those who already believe, this is one of the great shortcomings of the churches in our time. Evangelism is another, if this is to be understood as it often is, as "talking religion" to people who are not interested and who won't become so by evangelistic campaigns which create a moralistic type of Christianity for people who want to feel good and who want to do good.

Christianity is entirely different from any moralistic enterprise. It has to be lived existentially, as Bonhoeffer did and wrote.[3] Christianity has to learn that the world of today has become mundane (what Bonhoeffer called *die muendig gewordene Welt*) and that the church, that Christianity has to serve the world in a very realistic way.[4] Thus Communism, in its attempt to rule the history of the twentieth century, can become our very challenge.

Let it not be misunderstood as if I were saying that because Communism tries to solve our contemporary problems, in whatever way, Christianity should do this in a better way. All we ought to be concerned about is that Christianity should, knowing and facing the facts, be contemporary, much more aware of the problems of our time and able to meet them more realistically; acting and witnessing accordingly. Thus, it would not give Communism the opportunity it has, in India, and in the younger nations of Africa, to meet the needs of the people according to the Communist ideology, expecting people to return thanks by conversion.

The fire is hot.

Where are the firemen?

3. See Bonhoeffer, *Prisoner for God*.
4. Bonhoeffer, *Prisoner for God*, 145–49, 158–64, 168–69.

It is wise to live with this question in an attempt to answer it by action, without the immaturity of merely being emotional about it, as long as we believe that *Christus Victor Est*.

8

The Christian Answer to Communism[1]

John Howard Yoder

The topic assigned to me is by no means a new one. The newspapers, the church papers, and our radio waves are full of Christian answers to Communism. Usually the answer is quite clear and quite simple. It is that our nation is God's nation, and we need simply to do more intensively what we have been doing. The opponents of our nation—meaning primarily in our day the communistically-inclined portions of the world—are evil; they may in fact be equated with the work of Satan in the world. Any method we as a nation can use to oppose those nations is God's method. If we have the slightest reason to suspect that Communism is involved, we as a Christian nation have no hesitation in replacing a government in Guatemala which does not please us. We are only ashamed that we were not able to do the same thing in Cuba. We are ready to make an alliance with anyone, even a dictator like Franco, as long as he is against the people we are against, because our cause is God's.

But it isn't. Only the most childish kind of provincialism can permit us to act on the assumption that our nation is a Christian nation.

The Answer Is Repentance

The first basic point I should like to make is that the Christian answer to Communism is a repentant answer. It does not consist in saying that "we" have only to do more earnestly, and more sacrificially what we have

1. A chapel talk at Goshen College, May 2, 1961, first published in the *Gospel Herald* 54.34.

already been doing; that our goals are the right ones; that we need only to pursue them with more vigor. Nor is the ground of our repentance merely that we have prayed to little or given too little for missions. Our offense is much deeper.

The Christian answer to Communism must be a repentant answer because Christians have broken the promises the Gospel makes. Communism is the result of and an example of this infidelity of Christian civilization when measured by the faith it confesses.

There Is in the Gospel a Promise of Social Leveling

We think at once of Isaiah describing the kind of fast that Jehovah wants: "Is not this the fast that I choose: to loose the bonds of wickedness, to undo the thongs of the yoke, to let the oppressed go free, and to break every yoke? Is it not to share your bread with the hungry, and bring the homeless poor into your house?" (Isa 58:6–7a).

The Old Testament law, although we do not know that it was kept faithfully, provided that every fifty years on the so-called "year of Jubilee" there should be a general reorganization of landholding, because the land belongs to Jehovah. Nor is this one of those parts of the Old Testament done away with by the New. In a very strange place, in the song of Mary, the annunciation of the coming birth of the Messiah, she praises God because: "He has put down the mighty from their thrones, and exalted those of low degree; he has filled the hungry with good things, and the rich he has sent empty away" (Luke 1:52–53).

Once the Christian church was well on its way, we find even stronger words: "Come now, you rich, weep and howl for the miseries that are coming upon you. Your riches have rotted and your garments are moth-eaten. Your gold and silver have rusted, and their rust will be evidence against you and will eat your flesh like fire. You have laid up treasure for the last days. Behold the wages of the laborers who mowed your fields, which you kept back by fraud, cry out; and the cries of the harvesters have reached the ears of the Lord of hosts" (Jas 1:1–4).

There is thus in the Christian message an unmistakable promise of social leveling. A former archbishop of Canterbury, William Temple, a man certainly not to be accused of Communism, has rightly called the Christian faith—with Judaism of course in its background—the most materialistic of all religions. Only the Christian faith has dared to proclaim that it is God's will that no man should be hungry.

The issue which separates us from Communism is thus not the question of a form of property-holding. It is not a question of "materialism" if thereby we mean the belief that men act as they do for material motives. Jesus said that long before Marx. It is whether we as Christians have the creative drive to bring into existence the kind of human fellowship that the gospel calls for. And this we have not done. Where a degree of social leveling has come in the West, it has been the result not of the direct Christian critique of social injustice, but of the forces of secularism and of humanism.

We Have Failed to Keep the Promise of the Gospel to Give Hope to Subject Peoples

True enough; there has been in our North American national heritages a certain vision of the ideal free society, "the patriots' dreams that see beyond. the years, the alabaster cities, gleam undimmed by human tears." But that is a secular vision. We do not feel that this vision is our contribution to Africa, or something we owe to the Chinese. It has become a selfish vision, only for us.

Christians Have Not Resisted the Common Human Temptation to Sanctify Our Means by Our Ends

We think of Stalin especially as a classical example of the willingness to do wrong that right may come of it, i.e., the willingness to accept almost any means, even the most inhuman, in order to obtain the ends which we have proclaimed to be good. But Stalin was only repeating what "Christians" had been doing all down through the history of Europe. The Inquisition was the invention of the church. The Crusades were a Christian institution. Nor was it only in the Middle Ages that the "Christian" West thus betrayed its ideals. Our journals have painted in lurid tones the pictures of the brutality of the repression of the uprisings in Hungary in 1956. But we have been told very little about the fact that our dear respected allies, the French, in the name of democracy and even in the name of Christianity, have committed more such brutalities every year in the last five years in Algeria than did the Russians in Hungary.

Christians Have Failed in Their Mission in That They Have Misused Their Religion as a Shelter for People in Privileged Positions

Remember the attitudes of industrialists toward their wealth, and of preachers toward the industrialists, in the early years of the Industrial Revolution. Marx was right. Religion was being used by its official spokesman as the opiate of the people. The poor were told to be happy with their lot; the rich were not told what the prophets say to the rich.

Christians Have Diluted the Gospel's Call to Personal Commitment

We all agree on principle that the gospel does call every individual to give himself in response to God's gift to man; and that this commitment which is called for by the gospel is to be personal and total. Yet this commitment has not been proclaimed as the gospel's demand in every age, and in every church, because we fear an appearance of self-righteousness if we say: "Here is the truth; join us. Here is the vision; give your life to it." We feel inwardly unsure; such a sweeping call to discipleship would seem immature; would be unbalanced; would be criticized as lacking in proportion and in perspective.

Sometimes we soft-pedal this call of the gospel for the reason which Martin Luther stated in a classic way, by saying simply that he feared the people wouldn't follow. We are afraid that if we ask too much, we cannot get people to accept our vision. But Communism which asks for more can get them. Marxism can call upon men for total commitment; can call upon them to take a path which means a kind of persecution, a kind of sacrifice, a kind of church discipline, for the sake of their vision of a kind of coming kingdom, and millions around the globe will give themselves to this as we are afraid to ask ourselves to give ourselves to our calling.

The Answer Is No Answer

The second basic point I would like to make is that the Christian answer to Communism is not an answer. The answer which our society is looking for, and which Communism expects to see set up over against itself, would be an alternative way to control the world, to organize society and to win over the neutral nations. This would be something which Christianity does not provide. It would be an alternative political and economic pattern to be advocated and sold to or even forced upon the rest of the world. It would be an ideology, a set of doctrines answering all our questions; telling us how things work and how we must behave; providing our youth with an instrument whereby our organization need have no more basic problems. The Christian message does not provide this for a society.

The answer to Communism which our world is looking for would assure our standard of living; would assure the stability of the society which we feel the Marxist movement around the world is threatening. Christian faith does not promise this. All of this—security, ideology, institutions—is the culture which men build; our society has built a culture around Christianity as other men have built theirs around other faiths. But cultures, societies, and even nations come and go, and the gospel will not stop this process.

The Answer Is Christ

What is then the Christian answer to Communism? It is first of all the cross. The cross frees man from the necessity to survive. The basic axiom of Marxist political philosophy is that one must be effective. This idea Marxists learned from the Christians, but it is an idea which is neither true nor Christian. We do not have to survive; we do not have to be effective. When Jesus was crucified, his acceptance of this path meant not only that he sacrificed himself; it meant that he sacrificed, as far as man could see, God's own cause. Discipleship frees us from the need to be effective. Yet Christ did not thereby abandon the earthly effectiveness of God's cause as incarnated in himself, for the cross was itself God's cause.

The Christian answer to Communism is the resurrection. The resurrection tells us that in the face of evil and ignorance we are not limited to the available possibilities. When all the doors are closed God opens a window. The meaning of the resurrection for men is that it is never true that there is no solution. God's possibilities go beyond the apparently available openings left for good by our society and our cultural situation.

The Christian answer to Communism is the proclamation of the ascension of Christ: Jesus shall reign! This means that already in our age, though we cannot see how, Christ is Lord over the course of history. This was one of the central themes of the proclamation of the New Testament church. We today seldom talk of this theme. Somehow, surprisingly, it was clearer to the New Testament church, in the midst of persecution, that Christ was ruling over pagan governments, than it is today for us with no persecution, and with our faith in fact being supported or favored by our government. Christians' confidence in the Lordship of Christ over history has been surest in the life of the church when this Lordship has been the least visible. The knowledge that Christ is Lord, that even now providentially he is guiding things that we cannot understand, and events that we cannot influence, for his purposes, frees us from the need to feel "responsible" for making things come out right; it joyfully liberates us from the pressure of thinking that the future of the world depends on us.

The Christian answer to Communism is the message of Pentecost. God has created in the world a new kind of human community. It is not the nation that he cares about most; not even the freedom-loving, peace-loving, prosperous nation. The new community provides not only a way to live together, but for the Christian church also a way of making decisions and of finding God's will in our age. We do not have to look for our guidance to a book, whether to *Das Kapital*; or to a childish effort to dig out of the Bible things that aren't there. We are led, with the guidance of the witness of the Bible, but also with the guidance of the Holy Spirit today, to find God's will in our lives. And this frees us from the need to think we have to organize everything. If God, the Holy Spirit, is actually working among men, then some things can get done without the approval of some central office. Perhaps some things might even happen rightly without General Conference's dealing with them.

Just because God has ways of working among men, the Christian answer to Communism is the proclamation of the return of Christ, which once again frees us from the need to meet our own deadlines. We know when the door for some kinds of church work closed in China. We might know when the door closes in Cuba. But we can't tell when the door is closing for the world, and it is not our assignment to work against that deadline. We must never short circuit our task in the world by saying, "We have only so many years; let us do it the short way, the easy way; let's use the big stick." We can use God's methods and can have confidence in using only God's methods, because the end of history will be fixed, not by Marxism's closing doors, not by one nation's collapsing or another nation's becoming all-powerful, but by the coming of the King.

Prayer

Deliver us, our Father, through the gift of Thy Spirit, once again in our day, from the compulsion to defend our past and our peoples and our prejudices. Grant us an understanding of the part which our infidelity has played in bringing into this world the ferment of the Marxist faith. Grant that we might see the world revolution of our age not as an enemy over against which we must sharpen and deepen our defensiveness and our search for security; but as one of those powers through whose working in the world the Lord of all history is still capable of fulfilling his purpose. Free us from the fear of losing control of things. Free us to serve in the way of the cross. For we ask it in his name who first of all let his holy cause be defeated for our sake. Amen.

9

Marginalia

John Howard Yoder

Professor Dr. Jan M. Lochmann is Professor for Systematic Theology in the Comenius Theological Faculty of Prague, member of the Presbyterian Church of Czech Brethren, Director of the Hus Seminar (i.e., student home) of the Faculty, and one of the leaders of the Christian Peace Conferences held in Prague in recent years, the most recent of which was the "All Christian Assembly" of June 1961. His article on "Christian Thought in the Age of the Cold War" was presented to one of the preparatory commissions of the "All Christian Assembly."

Albert Gaillard is a pastor in the Reformed Church of France and has recently become Secretary General of that Church. His last previous pastorate was in Toulouse. In recent years he was able to maintain personal acquaintance with numerous French Communists especially within the Peace Partisans movement. The present paper was presented at Bievres, France, in August 1960, to the Third "Puidoux" Conference on the Church and Peace.

Miss Katharina van Drimmelen is the director of "Den Alerdinck," a Protestant lay-training academy near Zwolle, Holland. During the past year she has been in the United States, traveling extensively in an ecumenical mission sponsored by the United Presbyterian Church. In between her numerous speaking engagements, she found time to write this article on the Christian attitude towards Communism. She writes on the basis of numerous personal visits to the East Zone of Germany. Miss van Drimmelen, a graduate in theology from Leyden University, has completed major studies at Selly Oak Colleges, Birmingham, England, and at New

College, Edinburgh. During seven years as the pastor of a rural church in northern Holland, she preached, led women's programs, officiated at marriages, visited and counseled the people—but she could not administer baptism and communion because the Dutch Synod did not ordain women. The lay academy which she directs was started in 1949, following World War II. At this critical time, the Dutch Reformed Church, seeking to meet the needs of its people, instituted a new church order, one of witness, to replace its confessional one that dated back to 1619. The church established several academies for training lay people in witness, and they called Miss van Drimmelen to head one of them.

The major articles in this issue of *Concern* are closely related, though more by context than by content, to a problem with which Christians in the United States find it exceptionally difficult to come to grips in a way befitting the gospel. Whatever may be said of the ravages of secularism and of the renewed vitality of the older world religions, it is still Marxism which represents for most men today the livest ideological option, the most likely bidder for the allegiance of the millions—though it be but a century old—and our age's most immediately effective political philosophy, though its political implementation dates only from 1917. Never in history has any religion, philosophy, or form of government brought half the world's population under its sway in less than a half century.

Marxism has been analyzed with great thoroughness by philosophers as a philosophy, by economists as an economic theory, and by political scientists as a form of government, but few theological analyses have gone far beyond vilification. In the English-speaking world, the recent works of Charles West are among the most encouraging. *Concern's* publishing the papers of Gaillard, Lochmann, and van Drimmelen is first of all a testimony that Western Christians must see more in Marxism than a diabolic bogeyman for frightening people into individual repentance or into supporting missions, or a reprehensible atheism which must be destroyed even if half of civilization be annihilated with it.

Marxism is a view of man, of history, of nature, and of morals. Like every other post-Christian ideology it is neither all right nor all wrong, but a mixture of truths and misapprehensions. Only someone utterly convinced that Christianity for its part has never made a mistake—i.e., only a convinced Roman Catholic—can by writing off the errors convince himself that there is no truth to be found. After introducing the three major papers we shall attempt to suggest some lines of further conversation toward an evangelical Christian view of Marxism.

For a millennium and one-half, the best efforts of Christian leadership have been devoted to the majestic vision of a "Christian civilization." This meant not only the alliance of church and state; it involved also, and more basically, the development of a worldview, expressed in social structures, in the arts, and in philosophy, founded expressly upon Christian presuppositions. This vision of "Christendom" has guided and inspired the bulk of Christian social thought, little shaken through the years by the critiques of religious minorities, and still sets today the dominant tone for most Christians in the West.

This is the attitude which Christians in our time must overcome, especially if living under pagan or Marxist sovereignty. The Lochmann article testifies to the depth of the effort of one such Christian to rethink the church's social witness and responsibility in this new light. Dr. Lochmann is Professor of Theology in the Comenius Ecumenical Theological Faculty of Prague and a leader in the Prague Christian Peace Conferences.

The Christian critique of society and culture at a given time and place will always inconvenience some parties in that society more than others; certain segments of a population, or certain nations, will therefore, for their own selfish reasons, occasionally find some parts of the Christian message to their liking. Jesus's message seemed for a time to fit into the designs of the Zealots: the adversary of militarism, of fascism, or of economic exploitation is always somehow "partisan."

Thus, it is clear that Prof. Lochmann's critique of the identification of Christian faith with a given culture or its "ideology" is aimed at a particular temptation of the "Constantinian" West; this has led to its being circulated by the "Christian Democratic" minority party of the (East) German Democratic Republic. When American preachers cease attacking their nation's enemies, we shall be in a position to ask Lochmann whether his criticism of a peculiarly Western weakness is impartially balanced. But even if this passing political acceptability of the Christian "peace message" in the East should be reprehensible, the fault lies with the West; for the only reason a Christian critique of belligerent patriotism seems to socialist rulers to be grist for their mill is that a crusading Christian patriotism has in fact been and still largely is typical of the West.

It is further a possible valid critique of the church, the Seminary, and the Peace Conference in which J. M. Lochmann is a leader, that they accept (primarily in the form of pastoral salaries) the support of a theoretically atheistic state for Christian activities. Yet once again the pattern of state support in Prague is a carryover from fifteen centuries of similar alliances of churches with all kinds of states in all kinds of causes; might such an uneasy, transitory conjuncture of interests as currently obtains between the Christian peace witness and Khrushchev's "co-existence" propaganda be a less dangerous kind of collaboration with the state than the unqualified and unquestioning Western acceptance of the statesman as "emergency bishop" (Luther) or "principal member" (Zwingli) of the church? Even were we to assume sweepingly (as we do not) that all statesmen in the People's Democracies are ogres, would it not be likely that the ogres' Christian subjects, persecuted yesterday and probably discriminated against tomorrow, when once given a breath of freedom because it suits their rulers, would run less risk of losing their spiritual independence than the court preachers in the other camp, whose theology has coincided for centuries with that of their rulers?

In making such a contrast, formal separation of church and state is of course not the question; ideological independence is. The American churches are thought to be separate from the state, yet the amount of church work financed by tax exemptions and deductions, clergy discounts and foundation grants is incalculable. A shift in the Internal Revenue regulations covering the deductibility of nominally designated gifts has led some American Church Agencies ("faith missions") to abandon procedures of accounting and support which they previously explained as being spiritually and theologically indispensable.

Thus far we have been discussing Lochmann's paper chiefly with reference to its context. Its content as well may call forth some reservations. Is it thus clear that the Christian faith is in no way an ideology? On this point the Barthian denial that Christian faith is a "religion" or "worldview" coincides with the pragmatic desire to avoid alienating the Marxist through a head-on clash of total world philosophies, because the Marxist is least free to respond as a human being when approached in this way. Yet the practical intent does not answer the question of principle; does not the gospel imply certain answers to the basic questions with which a "worldview" deals?

Logically one may distinguish two major questions which Marxism poses to the church: 1) What does Marxism as a philosophy, a religion, an ethic, signify for the Christian thinker? and 2) How should Christians under Marxist governments behave? Treating neither directly, Lochmann speaks to both questions. Freed from the urge to set up against the Marxism political philosophy a competing "Christian" political philosophy, Christians in the East will also be freed to contribute to the needs of their real neighbors rather than combatting a dead theory and maintaining a pro-Western fifth column.

Albert Gaillard, pastor and now administrator in the French Reformed Church, has in recent years had exceptional occasion to meet intellectually qualified Marxists; both Marxism and Protestantism are in France minorities enjoying the leadership of highly articulate analysts and spokesmen; Gaillard's argument needs no comment here beyond the reminder that his reporting, differing from that of most Westerners, is based on firsthand acquaintance with the thought of which he speaks. The same thing is true in the case of Miss Katharina van Drimmelen.

To encourage further thought and, if possible, articulate rebuttal, the following intentionally incomplete and overly pointed theses are submitted for examination. To some readers they may be scandalous; to others so self-evident that their elaboration is a waste of time. This great variety of convictions is both the cause and the effect of American Churchdom's fear of an open encounter with the dynamic of Marxist thought. Such fearful silence gives aid and comfort in the short run to the demagogues of the far right, and in the long run to Marxism itself, by nourishing the illusion that it can be overcome by the careful avoidance of the issues it raises and the world where it reigns.

Marxism Is a Humanism

The deep concern of Marx himself and of his followers is for the attainment of the good society, and their deep confidence is that men, once they are properly informed and organized, will be capable of building such a world.

It is thus a serious misapprehension to conclude from the label "dialectical materialism" that Marxism has no place for human liberty in either theory or practice (cf. on this point the Gaillard article). Materialism is not necessarily mechanism. As a mechanistic prediction of socio-economic evolution, Marx's vision of history has in fact been disproven by the successes of Communism. What the phrase "dialectical materialism" means to point to is the ineluctable certainty (based on faith) that the good society will triumph in the end. Psychologically this certainty is quite comparable to the New Testament expectation of the early Return of the Lord or of the Calvinist doctrine of Predestination; it undergirds rather than undermines personal moral commitment.

Similarly, it is a misapprehension to conclude from the brutality attendant on the coming-to-power of Communist regimes that a particularly crass "might-makes-right" attitude is intrinsic to the Marxist dream. In fact, Marxism, like no other political philosophy, has as its express purpose the elimination of the state. The inhumane methods used "provisionally" toward this visionary end need to be compared not with the visions of liberal democracy but with the reality of "Christian" war and government since Constantine, if our condemnation of violence is to keep its balance. If the atheistic purges of Stalin and Chou En-Lai are compared with the theistic Inquisition, and the Russian colonization of Eastern Europe with the record of France in Algeria and Portugal in Angola, or the treatment of the American Indians—and if the comparison takes account of the difference between the moral momentum of fifteen centuries of Christianization and five of Renaissance on one hand and on the other the two-generation shift from feudal to nuclear society which the world east of the Oder River is undergoing—we shall be surprised not at the authoritarianism and at the bloodiness of Communist rulers but at their respect for cultural traditions and "democratic" forms and their occasional willingness to adjust their theories to fit economic reality and their practices to respond to popular resentment.

Marxism Is Western

Few mental habits interfere more profoundly with accurate analysis than the popular opposition—current example in the writings of J. L. Hromadka as well as in the "West"—of "Marxist East" and "liberal" or "capitalist West." In reality, Marxism is only one more case of the intellectual and political colonization of Asia—and now Africa—by Europe. It reproduces with astonishing fidelity the basic deviations which differentiate, for example, Western from Eastern Catholicism and Catholicism from New Testament Christianity. Like the New Testament, Marxism sees a committed minority (the Party) as the mainspring of history, fulfilling the calling of the chosen but captive Israel (the working class); but like Rome and the Reformers, the function of the majority is not to suffer but to rule. Unlike the New

Testament, but like Western Christendom and its spiritual offspring fascism, Marxism seeks to fulfill history by its own efforts.

Marxism Is the Rod of God

When the people of God betray their unique calling, this is not a mere infraction of law; it is an interference with God's work in history, and its results—whether under the Old Alliance or even more under the New—can only be catastrophic. Apostate Christendom, sold to the alien gods Mars and Mammon, has only itself to thank for the rebellion of humanist dreamers against a church and an ideology which have broken all the promises of the gospel. Concretely, this means that we may as well accept the eventuality of Marxist world dominion as possible, or even probable, within a few decades.

The reason for this likelihood is not that socialism as an economic system is more efficient in meeting men's material needs. This assumption, though logically appealing to some, has not been proven, and if it is proven it will not be by the "East" but by Western Europe.

Fundamentally, the domination of the world by socialism is a possibility because of the moral drive of its heralds. Except perhaps in the Soviet Union and Czechoslovakia, the Communist Party is a "church," i.e., a militant, sacrificially committed, collectively disciplined minority convinced that time is on their side. But even outside this "church," in the younger nations attracted by the socialist ideal whole generations of students are convinced that work is worthwhile and that their efforts toward social betterment will be rewarded. In the short run, social effectiveness depends on conviction; the West, with pornography on the newsstands, indiscipline in the schools, early retirement as a vocational goal, and fear of lost privilege as a national purpose, is not ready to run.

Secondarily, Marxist ambitions will be furthered by the Western nations' having discredited their own ideals in Hiroshima, Suez, Little Rock, Angola, and Cuba. Many of these demoralizing blunders have arisen from the assumption that "democracy" is itself a product for exportation, under whatever pressure is needed, into all the younger nations. As a matter of fact, democracy is a fruit and not a plant; not a self-perpetuating growth but a rare and delicate after product of a long spiritual history. Democracy and the "free economy" can only survive where the general osmotic effect of the evangelical witness has created respect for individual and minority rights and a grasp of morality founded upon inner resources and not mere fear of punishment. Where the religious rootage of these virtues is absent in the population at large, they only can survive at all when a nearly ideal transition from colonialism leaves a country with exceptional cultural and political institutions (India), or where exceptionally rapid economic development gives enough wealth to share with all so that severe social rigidity and consequent class pressures do not develop (Brazil, Italy perhaps, Philippines). Lacking such rare fortune, orderly democracy has no long-range chance of getting rooted, and in the succession of tyrannies and coups d'Etat the other nations experience, the choices would seem to be:

a. a continuous succession of military coups, changing only the palace furniture, leaving administration in the hands of feudal lords and civil servants. This pattern, obtaining in Latin America and on the fringe of Asia, solves no social problems and creates no procedures or orderly succession, and is thus intrinsically unstable.

b. conservative authoritarianism, surviving by police methods and the planned braking of social change and economic progress. In the fanatic form (Hitler, McCarthy, the Algerian "ultras") self-defeating, this approach may survive several decades if used moderately yet thoroughly (Spain).

c. collectivist authoritarianism, sacrificing as far as necessary the individualist values of Western idealism, respecting them as far as possible for their value as propaganda and as methods of administration, this solution is more effective than a. because of its clear doctrine and authority, and more effective than both a. and b. because it favors rather than resisting or ignoring the forces of social change.

If the hungry masses are to decide, as in the long run they must, it will be only a matter of time until collectivist authoritarianism will have taken over all but a few island bastions where democratic pluralism has had an especially good chance and leans on a high degree of industrialization and rich natural resources. This is not a vague prediction; it is the self-evident prolongation of the revolution of our age, in which a third of a century sufficed for the collectivist wave to cover nearly half the world. There is nothing on the horizon—not even the Peace Corps—which gives any promise of stemming the tide. Preaching democracy as a political form, as the United States has felt conscientiously called to do in recent years, is not only no help; it actually draws attention away from the issues about which something could be done.

Marxism, Where Politically Dominant, Is to be Accepted by Christians as Constituting the "Higher Powers" of Rom 13

This thesis would have presented no difficulties to a New Testament Christian; yet for Western church people nourished by the vision of "Christendom" it is hard to swallow. The counter-assumption is that only a good government has a right to the subjection of its citizens, and that where a government is evil, atheistic, or unjust, the faithful should rebel, go underground, or emigrate. Protestant Christians in socialist countries are often looked on from the West as if their faithfulness could consist only in such withdrawal from their society. Yet Paul in Rom 13 was writing to a church under just such an unfriendly government. Our brethren in the "East" should make their homes there and let their light shine there; we should wish them well rather than asking them to be disloyal. We do not thereby approve of their government (any more than we do of our own) but we accept it. Just as seeing in Assyria "God's rod" (Isa 10) did not mean moral approval of a military campaign, so subjection to the powers that be is not bound to any judgment on the righteousness of what those powers do.

But not only in the West or in the past is the Church's hastily blessing her society reprehensible. Currently many church leaders in the younger nations, in an effort to testify to the Gospel's relevance for humanitarian and social concern, are drawn by a temptation to become the "court preachers" of the coming order as the Churches of Europe and America had been before. By undergirding theologically their peoples' strivings toward social welfare, national identity, and "Peace," they hope to burst out of the enclaves where western pietist missions or eastern orthodox liturgy have left them, proclaiming the redeeming relevance of the Kingdom of God for the deepest concerns of men.

So far so good; but beyond this need to meet men by speaking to their felt needs, fidelity to the Gospel demands an element of foreignness and of judgment as well. It would be tragic for the younger churches, right at the point where they seek to tear themselves away from the tutelage of the colonizers, to repeat the deepest error of Constantinian Christendom, its loss of critical and eschatological perspective over against its own society. After having experienced the minority status of the irrelevant "little flock" in the wrong way, our brethren in Prague and Bangalore may before they realize it become a "responsible" elite in an equally wrong way. A welfare state, a young, self-governing, hopeful state, is no exception from Rom 12. However idealistic the administrative elite, however constitutional its procedures, however many Christians there may be in Parliament and Cabinet (as there are in Czechoslovakia, Japan, Indonesia), the state is basically a structure of power struggle and not a welfare institution. Christians accept the "Powers that be" because they be, and not because what they do merits—or needs—a Christian blessing.

Part III
On Kingdom Economics
Articles from CONCERN 11 (1963)

10

Poverty[1]

Karl Barth

The word poverty is usually thought of in its sociological sense. It describes the state of a man who for one reason or another is lacking in, or is even entirely without, the material necessities of life; who, therefore, having to rely on the assistance—voluntary or other—of his fellows, has to do without a great many things. He may even have to go without those things most essential to him, which would be available had he adequate means. There are, however, also much to the fore in this world, still other instances of destitution and privation. Even a rich man can be poor in health. He can suffer from intellectual poverty, in contrast with which a poor man in the financial sense of the word may be rich. With all his wealth he may suffer from spiritual poverty and from poverty in his relations with those around him, whereas in comparison a financially poor man may be a veritable Croesus.

I have been asked, not for my own opinions, but for the Christian views on this subject. Therefore, I open my Bible and immediately light on the calm and almost disconcerting assertion that poverty, taken in the sociological sense—usual in this world —exists in this life of ours, has always existed, and will always exist. Although the Bible is certainly not lacking in pictures of material wealth, those who possess and enjoy such wealth can be seen at a glance to be really very "poor people." Throughout the Bible, however, the fact that there are both rich men and poor, in either sense of the word, appears to be a kind of divine ordering of events, which ordinance must serve

1. Reprinted from *Against the Stream* by permission of the Philosophical Library.

as a basis for all further thought—just as in this world we have to accept the fact of illness, war, and other human deeds of violence, without question and without concerning ourselves with ideas of an essentially "better future." Let us not rejoice or be angry too soon! Without that starting point in mind, however, we can comprehend nothing.

All the more striking is the fact which dominates the picture, namely, the unmistakable and definite sympathy towards poverty seen in the Old and New Testaments, also the sympathy with those who, according to that divine ordinance, in this life are poor in one way or another, but above all in the material sphere. If in accordance with God's will there are also rich people, if, especially in the Old Testament, he includes among his blessings the gift of riches to one man, he in no way takes up a neutral position between the poor man and the rich man. The rich may take care of their own future, he is on the side of the poor.

First, there is no place in the Bible where the rights of the rich are proclaimed, where God appears as the Lord and Savior of the rich and of their wealth, where the poor are exhorted to preserve the wealth of the rich and remain poor themselves merely for the sake of the rich. There are, however, many places in the Bible where the rights of the poor are proclaimed, where God declares himself to be the upholder and avenger of these rights, where the rich are commanded not to forget the rights of the poor, not to alter or ignore them just when they feel inclined to do so, but rather to be rich only for the sake of the poor and for their benefit. We cannot but recognize the high principles and radical spirit of the Bible on both of these questions.

Secondly, there is no place in the Bible where anything in the nature of praise is accorded to riches, where the rich are upheld and exalted. There are, however, many places where the poor are extolled as blessed, where they are called the chosen of God, where the words "the poor" are synonymous with "the righteous." The gospel was proclaimed to the poor, while on the contrary the rich are often shown in suspiciously close proximity to the mighty evildoers, whose pride goes before a fall. Because of their wealth they at least run a great risk.

They will not enter into the kingdom of heaven simply because they are rich men (just as a camel can hardly go through the eye of a needle, as we know), but to this end they must themselves sell all and become poor. In this respect the distinction made in the Bible is as sharp as a knife: the blessings of wealth cannot claim to be on an equal footing with the blessings of poverty.

Thus, the Bible is on the side of the poor, the impecunious and the destitute. He whom the Bible calls God is on the side of the poor. Therefore, the Christian attitude to poverty can consist only of a corresponding allegiance. This allegiance is, however, only the reflection, the likeness, the testimony of a much more comprehensive distinction. If one should wish to withdraw from that allegiance, then one cannot comprehend, or be in sympathy with, that all-embracing distinction to which it testifies. By "poverty" we—and the Bible too in these connections, which have already been mentioned—mean financial, or some such form of poverty as is found in this world. Why then does poverty stand thus illumined, and wealth lie in the shadows? It is possible to give two answers to this question:

First, because poverty as seen from the background of human existence, that is, from the point of view of the coming kingdom of God, and of the future life, is not a natural condition of life in this world but is part of the evil which dominates that life. It is perhaps the most striking result of human sin. God's ordinance, whereby the rich and the poor live together side by side, is only temporary. His coming kingdom will put an end to poverty.

Why then, should this end not be proclaimed here and now, since the word of God has already been heard? Why should God not here and now reveal himself to and dwell with those who suffer from this evil which has been ordained to disappear? Why should he not comfort and encourage the poor, simply because they are poor in this world, with the realization that their rights are the very mirror of his eternal justice. And why should he not give the rich of this world to understand anything other than that the rights of the poor—those who in this life are lacking in wealth and all things necessary—must be sacred to them for the sake of his righteous judgment and of the approaching release from poverty?

The other side of the question is this: that here and now not wealth but poverty is the mark of our present life and of the future kingdom promised to both rich and poor. For this kingdom is not still in the future but has come already. Christ was born: the Son of God, eternally rich, himself the source of fullness of life for everyone. But the kingdom is come in poverty because it is now become a reality to us men, who—rich or poor—are all greatly poverty-stricken in comparison with the abundant riches of the kingdom. Christ was born in poverty in the stable at Bethlehem, and he died in extreme poverty, nailed naked to the cross. He is, then, the companion, not of the rich men of this world, but of the poor of this world. For that reason, he called the poor blessed, and not the rich. For that reason, he is here and now always to be found in the company of the hungry, the homeless, the naked, the sick, the prisoners. For that reason, those who are rich must cleave to them, if they would be close to him. Therefore, in order that they themselves may be blessed, the rich must become poor, or at least in all earnest be ashamed of their wealth; if they have to part with that wealth, whether gradually or all of a sudden, they must not show surprise, nor horror, nor yet try to ward off poverty. Not wealth but poverty is the mark of heaven, the mirror of eternal salvation.

For Christ, in whom eternal salvation has come to those who in this world are rich or poor, is the Christ of poverty for all who are poor, all who are truly destitute and suffer any privation: such a one is the conqueror, who makes all poor men rich, and only such a one! In great humility did the most High God become the Lord of mankind. Man will have to follow the example of this humility, will have to confess his poverty, in order to grow rich in him.

One of Saint Paul's sayings sums all this up: "Ye know the grace of our Lord Jesus Christ, that, although He was rich, yet for your sakes He became poor, that ye through His poverty might be rich." That is, briefly, the Christian attitude to poverty.

11

The Poverty of Christ[1]

Andrew Murray

> Ye know the grace of our Lord Jesus Christ that, though He was rich, yet for your sakes He became poor, that ye through His poverty might be rich. (2 Cor 8:9)

"Through His Poverty": what does that mean? That he dispossessed himself of all heavenly and earthly possessions that the riches of earth and heaven might be ours? That he so took our place, as in our stead to walk in the path of earthly poverty, that we in comfort and ease might enjoy the heavenly riches he has won for us? Or has that "Through His Poverty" a deeper meaning, and does it imply that his poverty is the very path or passage that he opened up through which all must go who would fully enter into his riches? Does it mean that, just as he needed in poverty of spirit and body to die to the world that he might open for us the way to the heavenly treasures, so we need to walk in his footsteps, and can only through his poverty working in us, through fellowship with his poverty, come to the perfect enjoyment of the riches he came to bring? In other words, is the poverty of Jesus something for him alone, or something in which his disciples are to share?

There is scarce a trait in the life and character of Christ in which we do not look to him as an example—what are the lessons his holy poverty has to teach? Is the right to possess and enjoy the riches of earth, as it is now everywhere practiced in the church, part of what Christ has secured for us? Or, is it possible that the lack of faith in the beauty and blessedness of the poor life

---

1. Reprinted from the booklet *Money* by permission of Moody Press.

of Christ Jesus is part of the cause of our spiritual poverty; our lack of Christ's poverty the cause of our lack of his riches? Is there not a needs-be that we not only think of the one side, "For your sakes He became poor;" but as much of the other, "For His sake I suffer the loss of all things?"

In seeking an answer to these questions, we must first turn and gaze upon our blessed Lord, if maybe the Holy Spirit will unfold somewhat of the glory of this his blessed attribute. Unless our heart be fixed upon our Lord in patient and prayerful contemplation, and we wait for the Holy Spirit to give us his illumination, we may indeed have our thoughts about this Divine poverty, but we cannot really behold its glory, or have its power and blessing enter our life. May God give us understanding!

We must first of all see what the reason—the needs-be—was of the earthly poverty of Christ. He might have lived on earth possessed of riches, dispensing them with wise and liberal hand. He might have come in the enjoyment of a moderate competency, just enough to keep him from the dependence and homelessness which was his lot. In either case he might have taught his people of all ages such precious and much needed lessons as to the right use of the things of this world. What a sermon his life would have been on the far reaching words: they that buy as though they possessed not. But no, there was a divine necessity that his life must be one of entire poverty. In seeking for the explanation, we shall find two classes of reasons. There are those which have reference to us and his work for us as our Savior. There are others which are more closely connected with his own personal life as man, and the work the Father wrought in him, as he perfected him through suffering.

Of the reasons referring to his work, the principal ones are easily named. Christ's poverty is part of his entire and deep humiliation, a proof of his perfect humility—his willingness to descend to the very lowest depths of human misery, and to share to the full in all the consequences of sin. The poor have in all ages been despised, while the rich have been sought and honored: Christ came to be the despised and neglected of men in this, too.

Christ's poverty has ever been counted one of the proofs of his love. Love delights in giving, perfect love in giving all. The poverty of Christ is one of the expressions of that self-sacrificing love which held back nothing and seeks to win us for itself by the most absolute self-abnegation on our behalf. Christ's poverty is his fitness for sympathizing and helping us in all the trials that come to us from our relation to this world and its goods. The majority of mankind has to struggle with poverty. The majority of

God's saints have been a poor and afflicted people. The poverty of Christ has been to tens of thousands the assurance that he could feel for them; that, even as with him, earthly need was to be the occasion for heavenly help, the school for a life of faith, and the experience of God's faithfulness the path to heavenly riches.

Christ's poverty is the weapon and the proof of his complete victory over the world. As our Redeemer, he proved by his poverty that his kingdom is not of this world, that as little as he feared its threats or its death could he be tempted to seek help from its wealth or strength.

But these reasons are more external and official; the deeper spiritual significance of Christ's poverty will be disclosed as we regard it as part of his training as the Son of Man, and his exhibition of what the true life of man is to be.

Christ's poverty was part of that suffering through which he learned obedience and was perfected by God as our High Priest. To human nature poverty must ever be a trial. We were made to be kings and possessors of all things. To have nothing costs suffering.

Christ's human nature was not, as the Docetae taught, a mere appearance or show. There never was one so really, so intensely, a man as Christ Jesus: "true man of true man." Poverty implies dependence on others; it means contempt and shame; it often brings want and suffering; it always lacks the means and power of earth. Our blessed Lord felt all this as man. And it was part of that suffering through which the Father worked out his will in his Son, and the Son proved his submission to the Father, and his absolute trust in him.

Christ's poverty was part of his school of faith, in which he himself first learned, and then taught men, that life is more than meat, and that man liveth "not by bread alone, but by every word that proceedeth out of the mouth of God." In his own life he had to prove that God and the riches of heaven can more than satisfy a man who has nothing on earth; that trust in God for the earthly life is not vain; that one only needs as much as it pleases God to give. In his person we have witness to the power which comes with the preaching of the kingdom of heaven when the Preacher himself is the evidence of its sufficiency.

Christ's poverty was one of the marks of his entire separation from the world, the proof that he was of another world and another spirit. As it was with the fruit good for food and pleasant to the eye that sin entered the world, so the great power of the world over men is in the cares and possessions and enjoyments of this life. Christ came to conquer the world and cast out its prince, to win the world back to God. He did so by refusing every temptation to accept its gifts or seek its aid. Of this protest against the worldly spirit, its self-pleasing and its trust in the visible, the poverty of Christ was one of the chief elements. He overcame the world first in the temptations by which its prince sought to ensnare him, then, and through that, in its power over us. The poverty of Christ was thus no mere accident or external circumstance. It was an essential element of his holy, perfect life; one great secret of his power to conquer and to save; his path to the glory of God.

We want to know what our share in the poverty of Christ is to be, whether and how far we are to follow his example. Let us study what Christ taught his disciples. When he said to them, "Follow Me," "Come after Me, I will make you fishers of men," he called them to share with him in his poor and homeless life, in his state of entire dependence upon the care of God and the kindness of men. He more than once used strong expressions about forsaking all, renouncing all, losing all. And that they understood his call so is manifest from their forsaking nets and customs, and saying, through Peter, "We have forsaken all and followed Thee."

The call of Christ to come after him is often applied as if it were the call to repentance and salvation. This is by no means the case. The principles the call involves have their universal application; but, to expound and enforce them in truth, it is of great consequence first to understand the meaning of the call in its original intention. Christ separated for himself a band of men who were to live with him in closest fellowship, in entire conformity to his life, under his immediate training. These three conditions were indispensable for their receiving the Holy Spirit, for being true witnesses to him and the life which he had lived and would impart to men. With them, as with him, the surrender of all property and the acceptance of a state of poverty was manifestly a condition and a means without which the full possession of the heavenly riches in such power as to convince men of their worth could not come.

With Paul the case appears to have been very little different. Without any express command we know of, the Spirit of his Master so possessed him, and made the eternal world so real and glorious to him, that its expulsive power made every thought of property or position disappear. He learned to give utterance, as no one else ever could do, to what must have been our Blessed Lord's inmost life in the words he uses of himself: "as poor, yet making many rich; as having nothing, yet possessing all things."

And in his wonderful life, as in his writings, he proves what weight it gives to the testimony concerning eternal things when the witness can appeal to his own experience of the infinite satisfaction which the unseen riches can give. In Paul, as in Christ, poverty was the natural consequence of an all-consuming passion, and made him a channel through whom the Invisible Power could flow full and free.

The history of the church tells us a sad story of the increase of wealth and worldly power, and the proportionate loss of the heavenly gift with which she had been entrusted, and which could alone bless the nations. The contrast to the apostolic state is set in the clearest light by a story that is told of one of the popes. When Thomas Aquinas first visited Rome and expressed his amazement at all the wealth he saw, the Pope said, "We can no longer say, 'Silver and gold hove I none.'" "No, indeed," was the answer, "nor can we say, 'What I have that give I thee. In the name of Jesus Christ of Nazareth rise up and walk.'" The earthly poverty and the heavenly power had been closely allied, with the one the other had gone. Through successive ages the conviction ever came that it was only by a return to poverty that the bonds of earth beneath would be broken and the blessing from above brought back, and many a vain attempt was made to secure to poverty a place in the preaching and practice of the church such as it had been in Pentecostal days. At times, the earnest efforts of holy men met with temporary success, soon to give way again to the terrible power of the great enemy—the world.

There were various reasons for this failure. One was that men understood not that in Christianity it is not an external act or state that can profit, but only the spirit that animates. The words of Christ were forgotten: "The Kingdom of God is within you;" and men expected from poverty what only the Spirit of Christ, revealing itself in poverty, could accomplish. Men sought to make a law of it, to bind under its rules and gather into its brotherhoods, souls that had no inner calling or capacity for such imitation of Christ. The church sought to invest poverty with the mantle of a peculiar holiness, and by its doctrine of Counsels of Perfection to offer a reward for this higher perfection. She taught that, while what was commanded in the gospel was the duty of all, there were certain acts or modes of living which were left to the choice of the disciple. They were not of binding obligation; to follow these counsels was more than simple obedience, a work of supererogation which therefore had special merit. Out of this grew the doctrine of the power the church has to dispense this surplus merit of the saints to those who were lacking. And, in some cases, poverty became only a new source of self-righteousness, entering into covenant with wealth, and casting its dark and deadly shadow over those it promised to save.

At the time of the Reformation, poverty had become so desecrated as a part of the great system of evil it had to combat, that, in casting out those errors, it cast out part of the truth with them. Since that time, it is as if our Protestant theology has never ventured to enquire what the place and the meaning and the power is which Christ and the apostle really gave poverty in their teaching and practice. And even in our days, when God is still raising up not a few witnesses to the blessedness of giving up all to trust in him, and of possessing nothing that one may possess him the more fully, the church can hardly be said to have found the right expression for its faith in the Spirit of Christ's poverty, as a power that is still to be counted as one of the gifts he bestows on some of its members. It will be found that there is no small difficulty in trying to formulate the teaching of Scripture so as to meet the views of Evangelical believers.

I have spoken above of the errors connected with the teaching of the Counsels of Perfection. And yet there was a measure of truth in that teaching, too. The error was to say that the highest conformity to Christ was not a matter of duty, but of option. Scripture says, "To him that knoweth to do good and doeth it not, to him it is sin." Wherever God's will is known, it must be obeyed. The mistake would have been avoided if attention had been paid to the difference of knowledge or spiritual insight by which our apprehensions of duty are affected. There is a diversity of gift and capacity, or spiritual receptivity and growth, of calling and grace, which makes a difference, not in the obligation of each to seek the most complete inner conformity to Christ, but in the possibility of externally manifesting that conformity in such ways as were seen in Christ.

During the three years of his public career, Christ gave himself and his whole time to direct work for God. He did not labor for his livelihood. He chose for himself disciples who would follow him in this, forsaking and for direct work in the service of the kingdom.

For admission to this inner circle of his chosen ones, Christ demanded what he did not from those who came seeking only salvation. They were to share with him in the work and the glory of the new kingdom; they must share with him in the poverty that owns nothing for this world.

From what has been said above, it is clear that no law can be laid down. It is not a question of law, but of liberty. But we must understand that word "liberty" aright. Too often Christian liberty is spoken of as our freedom from too great restraint in sacrificing our own will, or the enjoyment of the world. Its real meaning is the very opposite. True love asks to be as free as possible from self and the world to bring its all to God. Instead of the question, "How free am I, as a Christian, still free to do this or the other?" the truly free spirit asks, "How far am I free to follow Christ to the uttermost?" Does the freedom with which Christ hath made us free really give us the liberty, in a love which longs for the closest possible likeness and union with him—still to forsake all and follow him? Among the gifts and calling he still dispenses to his church, will there not be some whom by his Spirit he still draws in this particular, too, to bear and show forth his image? Do we not need as much as when he and his apostles were upon earth, men and women to give concrete and practical evidence that the man who literally gives up all of earthly possession because he sets his heart upon the treasure of heaven, can count upon God to provide for the things of earth?

Is not this, amid the universal confession of worldliness in the church and the Christian life, just the protest that is needed against the so subtle but mighty claim that the world makes upon us? In connection with every church and mission and work of philanthropy the question is asked, "How is it that in Christian countries hundreds of millions are spent on luxuries, with scarcely single millions for God's work?" Calculations are made as to what could be done if all Christians were only to be moderately liberal. I fear all such argument avails little. Help must come from a different direction. It was of the innermost circle that he had gathered around himself that Christ asked a poverty as absolute as his own. It is in the innermost circle of God's children, among those who make the highest profession of insight into the riches of grace and their entire surrender to it, that we must find the witnesses that his Spirit can still inspire and strengthen to bear his poverty. He has done it and is doing it. In many a missionary and Salvation Army officer, in many a humble unknown worker, his Spirit is working out this trait of his blessed likeness. In the days we are looking for of deeper revival among God's children, he will do it still more abundantly.

Blessed are all they who wait for him, to receive his teaching, to know his mind, and show forth his holy likeness. It is as the first, the inner, circle proves the power of his presence, that the second and the third will feel the influence. Men of moderate means, who may feel no calling to the poor life, will come under the constraining power of the example and feel compelled to sacrifice far more of comfort and enjoyment in Christ's service than they ever did before. And the rich will have their attention attracted to the danger signals God has set along their path,[2] and will, by these examples, if they may not themselves share in Christ's poverty, at least be helped to set their hearts more intensely upon the treasure in heaven—the being rich in faith, rich in good works, rich toward God—and to know themselves heirs of God, heirs of the riches of grace, and the riches of glory.

"That ye through His poverty might become rich." *His poverty*, not only as an object of our faith, but as a matter of experience and fellowship is the passage through which the fullest entrance is gained into his riches.

---

2. Luke 18:25; Matt 6:19–21; 1 Tim 6:9, 10, 17.

12

Money[1]

R. Mehl

Ideas of money, gold possessions, riches, Mammon, are closely associated in biblical thought. Possessions, or riches, is the term with the widest denotation. The term gold or silver does not signify on all historical levels of the Bible the symbolic realities which we designate by these names: they are often material things, precious in themselves and not as objects of exchange.[2]

Possessions, riches, gold, and silver constitute the splendor and the glory of the creation, and as the creation is never regarded as independent of the Creator that splendor and that glory belong to him (Ps 24:1). He disposes of them, he promises them and gives them to those he loves, freely, gratuitously, even when man in no way deserves it. So God promises to Moses for his people "great and goodly cities, which you did not build, and houses full of all good things, which you did not fill, and cisterns hewn out, which you did not hew, and vineyards and olive trees, which you did not plant" (Deut 6:11). Thus, riches are above all a sign of the blessing of God, of his free grace and his free election. They testify to the faithfulness of God, and the faithfulness of men to God is paid in return by means of possessions.[3] Even when given by God, possessions and riches must always still be regarded

---

1. Reprinted from von Allmen, *Vocabulary of the Bible*, with permission.

2. Gen 2:11–12 and Hag 2:7–8: "the treasures of all nations shall come in, and I will fill this house with splendor, says the Lord of hosts. The silver is mine, and the gold is mine, says the Lord of hosts."

3. Ps 34:10; 36:8; 65:9–13; Isa 1:19: "If you are willing and obedient, you shall eat the good of the land."

by man as belonging to God (Ps 105:24; Hag 2:7–8). He who inherits the promise must not forget that it is the Lord alone who promises and who gives and that he alone guarantees and assures the continuance of the possessions which he gives. It is not possible to dissociate the act of giving from the thing given, as Ps 16:5–6 shows: "The Lord is my chosen portion and my cup; thou holdest my lot. The lines have fallen for me in pleasant places; yea, I have a goodly heritage." All the history of Israel, so long as the people remain faithful, testifies to this concern of not appropriating in an absolute manner the gifts of God. He who continues to dispense them can take them back, as the book of Job clearly shows.

In addition, these goods and riches are regarded much more as sustenance which God gives to satisfy men who are hungry and thirsty (and to the degree in which they are hungry and thirsty) than as possessions to accumulate. The Old Testament stresses less the proprietary rights of man than the fact that man can enjoy what is given to him.[4] Man has the usufruct of creation; he is not its proprietor in the full sense of the term. God has created him to joy and rejoice in the good things of this earth. Doubtless this statement must be related to the kind of civilization and the mode of existence of ancient Israel: nomads or semi-nomads, they did not seek to accumulate possessions, they sought food, and the story of the manna with which God fed them in the desert left a profound memory in their tradition (Exod 16), since Paul can refer to it as a piece of fundamental teaching (2 Cor 8:15). But that explanation is not sufficient, because Israel became a settled, property-owning people and yet even then the accumulation of goods and wealth was not accepted without difficulties or scruples. At all events, such accumulation was always made the object of reprobation, especially by the prophets.[5] This accumulation calls forth the judgment of God, who will withdraw that which is his own (Zech 9:4). Furthermore, Deuteronomy shows us that Israel was conscious of the spiritual danger attached to sedentary life, to the possession of a soil and a kingdom: and so the accumulation of horses, of wives, of gold and silver is clearly forbidden to the king (17:16–17), and in spite of all his wisdom and piety King Solomon will be blamed for having made "silver as common in Jerusalem as stone" (1 Kgs 10:27), and the downfall of Solomon's kingdom is connected with that policy of accumulation made worse by his successor (1 Kgs 12). In

---

4. See for example Eccl 5:18–20.

5. Compare Ezek 27 and 28: the city of Tyre is accursed because of the accumulation of its riches and its trade.

the eyes of the Old Testament it is the unique lordship of God, the Creator and Father, which is challenged by any policy of accumulation or avarice: these things represent mistrust of God.

The New Testament, which underlines less strongly than the Old Testament, the idea that earthly goods are the sign of God's blessings takes up with much energy, on the other hand, the forbidding of the appropriation of goods which belong to God only.[6] This appropriation marks our intention of dispensing with God (the parable of the rich fool (Luke 12:15–21), or our inability to follow Jesus Christ.[7] James stresses that there is no appropriation of riches which is not associated with some injustice (5:1–6). Similarly, 1 John 3:17 establishes an incompatibility between the possession of goods and brotherly love. A veritable duty of improvidence is recommended by 1 Tim 6:17–19: spiritual foresight consists, on the contrary, in generously distributing one's goods, by putting them at the disposal of those in need. So the final worth of all riches is to meet the needs of those who are hungry. The good things of creation are not intended to be accumulated or to insure the power of a man; they are indeed "consumer goods." The rich man who egotistically keeps his possessions to himself is accursed, whilst the poor man is called happy (Luke 6:20). This explains the attitude of the first Jerusalem community: the sharing of all the money after the sale of their possessions (Acts 2:45 and 4:32). The possessions are for the poor, not in order that they may become rich in their turn, but that their misery may cease; and it would not conform to the spirit of the Bible to take these words of the Magnificat only in a spiritual sense: "He has filled the hungry with good things, and the rich he has sent empty away" (Luke 1:53). This collection of texts must not be regarded as a eulogy on poverty itself; the condition of misery is not agreeable to God. On the contrary, God wishes it to cease, and that is why he forbids the accumulation of possessions in the hands of the rich. That accumulation announces the ruin of the rich man, who puts his confidence not in God but in his riches themselves.

The idea that these constitute a favor of God and a blessing is not lost sight of in the New Testament, but it is connected with the idea of renunciation. A man must lose his life to gain it: "Truly, I say to you, there is no one who has left house or brothers or sisters or mother or father or children or

---

6. Luke 15:12, the parable of the prodigal son, in which one sees that the claim and the appropriation signify separation from God.

7. See for example the story of the rich young man: the young man "went away sorrowful: for he had great possessions," Matt 19:22.

lands, for my sake and for the gospel, who will not receive a hundredfold now in this time, houses and brothers and sisters and mothers and children and lands, with persecutions, and in the age to come eternal life" (Mark 10:29–30). It will be observed, however, that earthly blessings do not constitute an absolute and unequivocal sign of divine grace: in the middle of all these possessions persecutions also find a place. The Old Testament had already shown that possessions are not an absolute criterion, and unimpeachable proof of the favor of God, for "better is a little that the righteous have than the abundance of many wicked" (Ps 37:16), and Job struggled for a long time to arrive at the certainty that his wretchedness and misery were not proof of his abandonment by God.

Whilst it is true that the concept of possessions includes that of money and that all that has been said about the former could be repeated of the latter, nevertheless money merits a study of its own because more than other possessions it represents a menace to man. "The love of money is the root of all evils" (1 Tim 6:10). The token of money, by the facilities which it offers a man, enormously increases his power and excites in him a passion without limits: "He who loves money will not be satisfied with money; nor he who loves wealth, with gain" (Eccl 5:10). In a certain sense it is the opposite of a good thing meant to supply a need: it does not satisfy but multiplies the will to power. It constitutes for man a permanent source of bondage. That is why the Mosaic legislation was so concerned to limit the power of money: the prohibition of the taking of interest on loans and of usury in so far as the relations of Israelites between themselves and of Israelites and strangers living in their territory are concerned.[8] Very properly the Old Testament fears that money might intrude itself between a man and his neighbor and impair their relationship. One could compare all these prescriptions with those which deal with wages,[9] for they also testify to a concern not to let money acquire a power of oppression. James (2:1–4) reminds us that the consideration given to people because of their wealth and the external signs of wealth leads to discriminations which ruin all brotherliness. But it is Jesus above all who throws into relief the demonic power of money and possessions.

By a kind of fatality, a man places his confidence in them, and it is then impossible for him to enter into the kingdom of heaven (Mark 10:23–25). Jesus will therefore demand a radical renunciation of the power of money:

---

8. Deut 23:20; Lev 25:35, 36; Exod 22:25.
9. Deut 24:14–15; Jer 22:13, cf. Jas 5:4.

"Sell your possessions, and give alms; provide yourselves with purses that do not grow old, with a treasure in the heavens that does not fail, where no thief approaches and no moth destroys. For where your treasure is, there will your heart be also" (Luke 12:33–34). It must be observed that this precept of Jesus is inserted in a sequence on eschatological expectancy of the kingdom: money, and the cares which attach to every form of possessions, deprive us of that openness of mind and that liberty which are necessary in the search for the kingdom. Money alienates us both from the kingdom and from hope. There lies its omnipotence. Contrary to what modern man thinks, the power of money does not come solely from an inward passion which may devour us. That inward passion, the reality of which Jesus never disregards, corresponds to an outward and objective reality. Money is not a neutral thing which may offer itself for the good or bad use which we may make of it. In the eyes of Jesus, money takes its place among the demonic powers which enslave man. That is why he gives it a demonic name, Mammon (Matt 6:24; Luke 16:13). J. Ellul writes:

> It is known that it is a question here of an Aramaic word which means in general money, and which can also signify wealth. Here Jesus personifies Money and regards it as a kind of god. Now, this is by no means derived from contemporary usage. Jesus has not taken a denotation current amongst the people He was addressing, for it does not seem that a god of this name was known amongst Jews and Galileans or amongst the neighboring Gentiles. Jesus does not seek a pagan deity to show that one must choose between the true God and a false god. He certainly does not refer to a current superstition which He might have more or less shared. This personification of money appears to be a creation of Jesus Himself, and, if such it is, it means that He reveals to us something exceptional, since Jesus does not customarily use these deifications and personifications.[10]

What Jesus shows us is precisely that supernatural power which money exercises over man, a power which, within the limits permitted by God himself, can hold God in check, a power which can be put alongside that of God. Hence the dilemma: "No one can serve two masters. . . . You cannot serve God and Mammon" (Matt 6:24). Only the lordship of him who "disarmed the principalities and powers and made a public example of them, triumphing over them by the cross" (Col 2:15) can set a limit to the lordship

---

10. Ellul, "L'argent," 31, author's translation.

of Mammon, just as it puts a limit to every care and every anxiety. The Old Testament had already noticed where this power of money could lead. Amos (2:6) denounces the crimes of the children of Israel who "sell the righteous for silver, and the needy for a pair of shoes." Mic (3:11) describes in these terms the perversion of the house of Israel: "Its heads give judgment for a bribe, its priests teach for hire its prophets divine for money." The same phenomena are described by the New Testament: it is the lust for money which drives men to transform the house of prayer into a house of trade (John 2:16). Ananias and Sapphira break the fellowship of the Church through the love of money (Acts 5:2); Simon the magician—and it is not without importance to underline that he is a man who has dealings with demoniacal powers—believes that the gift of God is acquired by money (Acts 8:20); Felix expects from Paul, not the word of salvation, but money merely (Acts 24:26). Finally and above all, the word of Amos becomes a kind of prophecy which is fulfilled in Judas (Mark 14:11) and in the soldiers whose false witness against the resurrection is achieved by money (Matt 28:12–13). It is very striking that amongst all the demonic powers which joined together so that the Son of God should die on the cross, money had its place and even played a decisive part. For he who was crucified is the Righteous One, but money is designated by Jesus with the name of "unrighteous mammon" (Luke 16:11). There could be no compromise there between the Righteous One and Mammon. This is why Jesus refused to protect with his authority the power of money: it is necessary to render to Caesar (i.e., to another power) the money which belongs to him (Matt 22:21). Money as such cannot be put at the service of God.

To the constraining power of Mammon there will then be opposed the gratuitousness of the word and of the kingdom; the liberation of man is not gained by payment of money: "Come to the waters; and he who has no money, come, buy and eat . . . without money and without price" (Isa 55:1–2). The Twelve will be sent on a mission without money (Mark 6:8). Paradoxically, men will be fed, revived and saved by the Poor one: "For you know the grace of our Lord Jesus Christ that though he was rich, yet for your sake he became poor, so that by his poverty you might become rich" (2 Cor 8:9). The servant of Christ will therefore be a man who, without possessing any of the riches for which men thirst, will nevertheless enrich them. Consider the healing of the lame man at the Beautiful Gate by Peter: "I have no silver and gold, but I give you what I have: in the name of Jesus Christ of Nazareth walk" (Acts 3:6).

However, it is not permissible to conclude from these indications that the New Testament, repudiating the affirmation of the Old Testament according to which riches are a sign of the blessing of God, has forbidden believers to have any contact with money and has sanctioned an ethic of contempt for money: it is necessary to render to Caesar the money which belongs to him and Caesar must use it to accomplish a mission which, though transitory, is none the less in conformity with the will of God. To him who truly recognizes the lordship of Christ, money has lost its power. It could be said that the teaching of Jesus tends to devalue money: what counts is not money as such, its mere bulk, but the ability to dispose of it freely. Then money can become the object of an offering made to God himself (Mark 12:41–44: the widow's offering). Money can become the token of brotherly fellowship, as it is seen in the "communism" of the early church and as it is confirmed on the occasion of the collection for the Jerusalem church, a collection which was one of the chief signs of the church's unity. It is in the degree that money is freely given, and not amassed, that it is a blessing of God (1 Tim 6:18–19).

Contempt of money is by no means recommended. It is simply that money as a power must vanish before the power of Christ, that it must cease to be a power in order to become the sign of brotherly love. Paul gives a very concrete maxim which characterizes the new state of things: money as a power led to the enslaving of man by man, now it is going to lead to the re-establishment of equality between men. "I do not mean that others should be eased and you burdened, but that as a matter of equality your abundance at the present time should supply their want, so that their abundance may supply your want, that there may be equality" (2 Cor 8:13–14).

But it is above all the singular parable of the unfaithful steward (Luke 16:1–13) which clearly shows this dethronement of money as a power and its use for displaying the free salvation of God: the steward, although unfaithful and dishonest, is praised by Jesus and presented as a pattern because he took no account of the sacredness of money, but in the first place he regarded the distress of the debtors. Money is subordinate to man (insofar as it is subordinate to Jesus Christ) and it is better to make friends than to follow the religion of money. The point of this parable is therefore to proclaim that the money king is dethroned. Similarly, in the parable of the workmen hired at different hours of the day, the master shows that he cares less about respecting the laws imposed under the reign of money than of doing good to those he loves (Matt 20:1–16).

Far from recommending an ethic of abstention with regard to money and other forms of wealth the Bible invites man, during the absence of the Master (Matt 25:14) to use them, make them bear fruit (parable of the talents, vv. 14–30), and to use them to sustain men (Matt 24:45–47). But manifestly they can only do this if money has ceased to be a power, that is, if they themselves are Christ's (1 Cor 3:22). If they act thus their works will not be destitute of meaning. God will one day take, in a form which they cannot at present know, those works achieved by "unrighteous wealth" and they will be included in the kingdom (Rev 21:24). For these works belong to the Lord, and God's declaration (Hag 2:8), "the silver is mine, and the gold is mine" has essentially an eschatological meaning.

13

God or Mammon

Virgil Vogt

Introduction

The drama of history unfolds before us. To both onlooker and participant alike, the events are often interesting and sometimes exciting. But the meaning of it all is often uncertain. Many times, it is only as we look back on the events of history that we can see what was actually taking place at each moment. Only in retrospect can we see the consequences of our actions, many times. And even then, we are often at a loss to understand the abiding significance of all that has happened.

It is this lack of understanding and the failure to know the meaning of the events in which we are currently involved which leads men so frequently to choose the wrong course of action. If they could only know at the time when decisions are being made what the long-range outcome of these actions will be, how often and how differently men would act.

A large part of the biblical message is directed to this very uncertainty. Again and again God has been good enough to step in and let us know the meaning of current events. The long-range results which could not be determined simply by observation and calculation, God has time and again revealed to men in this world. He has announced beforehand what shall be the outcome so that men need not be led astray by the false impressions of the moment.

The preaching of Jesus was an announcement of this kind. He went about proclaiming that "the Kingdom of God is near." This fact was far from evident to the ordinary observers of his day. The events leading up to this were unfolding before the men of that generation, but they did not have eyes to perceive it. The appearances of history gave a false impression. To them it seemed, not that the kingdom of God was near, but that life in this world was going on as usual.

But God was good enough to let mankind know ahead of time that the kingdom of promise was just around the corner. In view of this fact, a definite course of action was called for. "Repent and believe" was the call that went out with the announcement. Men were invited to reorient their lives towards the coming kingdom. They were invited to make a decision which ran contrary to the ordinary evidence of history and to risk their lives on the strength of God's revelation through Christ. Jesus was announcing a crisis in history which was not as yet self-evident. He told of an old era coming to an end and of a new era being introduced by God. The reign of God in righteousness and truth was breaking in upon the common life of man. He invited men to receive this new state of affairs by becoming participants in it.

In the events of Good Friday, Easter, and Pentecost the critical turning point of history was passed. The thing which Jesus announced was realized. Not all was as yet fulfilled, but all the decisive events had taken place. What had existed only as announcement, graciously given by God, now existed as a realized fact in human history.

In these events, as in the coming of Jesus itself, God not only announced but actually accomplished his redemptive will for the world. This too is the constant theme of the Bible history. God not only reveals what men do not know, but he also does what man is unable to do. The men who know what to do but who find themselves unable or unwilling to do it are very much a part of the human situation.

What God did in Christ is also the solution to this dilemma. Here we see God taking the side of man and bringing to pass all those important events which man by himself had failed to reach. Now in and through these victories won by Jesus Christ all those men of faith who accept him enter into the legacy of blessing which is thereby created.

There are few areas of life in which the misleading impressions of the moment and the unsanctified wisdom of unbelievers are more wrong than in dealing with money. In this realm the words and actions of Christ do surely shine as light in the darkness.

In the pages that follow I will attempt to review some of the astonishing things which Jesus revealed about the true understanding and use of money and possessions. We cannot in this limited context say much about the setting in which such considerations must be understood. Very little can be said here about the community of faith in which the Holy Spirit is the basic source of counsel and power. We do not have space to describe the process by which one enters this realm of salvation nor the changes which occur in his experience. We cannot detail in this paper the relationship of priority which exists between grace and obedience within God's economy of redemption. Nor can we say much about where we stand in the total unfolding of the history of redemption which started in earnest with Abraham and the Exodus from Egypt and reached its glorious climax in the person and work of Jesus. We can only affirm at the outset that everything said in the paper is misunderstood if it is not seen in this context.

Accumulating Possessions

> Do not lay up for yourselves treasures on earth . . . for where your treasure is, there will your heart be also. (Matt 6:19, 21)

In these words, Jesus simply reverses the world's whole approach to economic life. Almost everywhere in the world today the accepted philosophy of life is that a man's life does indeed consist in the abundance of the things which he possesses. According to this point of view, it is a nice thing to have $10 in your pocket. But it is better to have $100 in the bank. And it is better still to have $1,000 or $10,000 in the bank. It is a good thing to have an eighty-acre farm, but it is better to have 160 acres, and better still to have 240. This is the standard by which most men live, and they are ready to pour out their lives to increase the number of their possessions.

In recent years we can, of course, observe a certain change in the way this principle is applied. Our fathers and grandfathers were concerned primarily about increasing capital goods. They devoted themselves to the purchase of farms or to carefully building up a savings account. Many of them were noted for the careful management, conservation and increase of their capital resources. And there are still many people in our day who live like this. But a younger generation has grown up in the midst of prosperity and these young people are more interested in consumer goods than in capital accumulation. They would rather have a new car every year or two as young people, than to drive an older model and put the money away for investment purposes. Many young families would rather spend $30,000 on a new home than to invest it in a farm, or in some business.

While this shift in emphasis has revolutionized the American economy, we must be careful to notice that the basic philosophy has not been changed. The age-old rule of life is unchallenged. People today, young as well as old, still believe that the more you have of this world's goods the better it is. In the old days a man wanted two farms, today he wants two cars. Instead of adding a new investment, the young modern family will probably add a new boat, a swimming pool, or a cottage at the lake. But this is only a different way of doing the same thing—laying up treasures on earth.

The Christian however, can have no part of this. His face is set in another direction, indeed, in the opposite direction. Jesus himself, by his own word and example, has reversed the Christian's whole outlook on economic life.

From Jesus the Christian has learned that the increase of one's possessions is not a blessing to be sought after. Rather it is something to be avoided. Instead of seeking to lay up treasure on earth, Jesus told his disciples they should be deliberate in not laying up treasure on earth. Instead of thinking that the more one has the better it is, the Christian understands that getting along with a reasonable minimum is to be preferred. The reasons for this will be made clear as we go along. At this point it is enough simply to observe what a complete change in outlook Jesus introduced into the realm of economics when he said, "Do not lay up treasure for yourself on earth." Only in this way can we be set free from the shackles which bind other men into economic bondage.

The Reasons For This Approach

In order that his counsel might commend itself, Jesus gives us, in Matt 6, the reasons which lie back of this unusual reversal of economic principles. He wants to make it clear that this is no arbitrary demand. Rather this is a profound insight into the inner dynamics of human experience.

His first remark is about *futility*. He said, why bother to lay up treasure on earth when something or someone is sure to take it away from you again. Either thieves, tragedies, or decay (and we would add taxes, depressions, inflations, and death) will take it away. The treasures which have been so carefully gathered together are sure to be scattered. There is no way to avoid this. It is only a question of time. So what's the use of gathering so many possessions?

Like the rich man of the Old Testament, Jesus is saying it is a "vanity of vanities. "What does a man gain by all the toil at which he toils under the sun? ... As he came from his mother's womb he shall go again, naked as he came, and shall take nothing for his toil. ... All streams run to the sea, but the sea is not full; to the place where the streams flow, there they flow again. All things are full of weariness" (Eccl 1:2, 3; 5:15; 1:7–8).

In this world of economic uncertainties and unexpected reversals, in this world of greed and competition, of depreciation and death, why would any sensible man pour out his soul to accumulate a few treasures which shall in but a brief moment be snatched away from him? Why not, as Jesus suggests, invest one's life energies in things that shall remain. Do not labor, he says in John 6:27, for things which perish but for that which endures to eternal life. Everyone who seeks to lay up treasures on this earth is doomed to futility.

Some time ago a retired farmer in Indiana received a rude awakening to this truth. $15,000 of the life savings of this eighty-two-year-old man were stolen from a metal cash box which he had hidden in an outdoor cellar behind his home. And why would an eighty-two-year-old man keep that much money in a box in his cellar? Because during the depression of 1929, he had lost a considerable sum of money through bank failures. When he kept it in the bank it was lost through economic reversals. So he put it in his fruit cellar where it could be kept safely. But when he kept it there, the thieves took it away. If thieves had not broken in death would soon have separated this man and his treasures. This is but a sample of the bitter and inevitable disappointment which has come or will come to every man who seeks to lay up treasures on earth.

Jesus warned that those who seek to accumulate many possessions are doomed to this kind of frustration. The forces of nature and humanity have conspired against them. Their purpose will always be defeated, and the cherished goal of their life will be snatched away from them. His counsel was simply to forsake this aimless striving.

A second reason concerns *the heart*. "Where your treasure is, there your heart will be also." This is a universal fact of human experience. Men are attached to their treasures. Possessions exercise a strange attraction for the loyalties of men. That is why the Christian who lays up treasure on earth is not only wasting his time, he is also endangering his own salvation. Jesus counseled against accumulating many possessions because he knew that man's heart is always drawn towards the things he possesses and that as possessions increase so the attraction increases.

We read in 1 Tim 6, that "the love of money is the root of all kinds of evil." From this many have concluded that the specific amount of wealth a person has makes little difference. What matters, they say, is the attitude we take towards our wealth. It is true, as it says in 1 Timothy, that the real offense is in the attitude of affection or loyalty which one has toward money. This reminds us that the poor man can be as much the offender in this respect as the rich. Many poor people are as dearly attached to the few things which they do possess as are the rich to their many possessions. Other poor people hope for nothing so much as to become a little more wealthy. These people are as much in love with money as any rich man.

But while the poor may be as much in love with money as the rich, we cannot reverse this proposition and say that the rich can be as free from the love of money as the poor. This is made clear in the statement from Jesus, "Where your treasure is, there your heart will be also." First Timothy says that the love of money is the problem. Jesus understands it this way too, but he goes a step further. He says, those who have it, love it. Without qualification, he says that where treasure has been accumulated, there the heart's affections also turn. Thus, while the man without any earthly treasure may be in love with the treasures of earth, the person who has accumulated considerable earthly treasure is always in love with it.

Many people, especially professing Christians, try to deny this kind of attachment to their many possessions. However, these people would never have accumulated so many had they not believed, with the rest of the world, that to gain more is better. Money does not grow on trees, neither do people become rich without much hard work and careful planning (except in certain rare cases). In this they simply reveal what Jesus said about affection for treasures of earth. Or again, if people with many possessions were not in love with them, they would not so carefully keep all those things for themselves but would freely share with others. In a world where thousands are starving and where many have never yet heard the message of Christ, no one who does not love his possessions will hang on to them. In spite of all their protests, the rich are attracted to their wealth. Where the treasure is, there will the heart be also.

While accepting the full validity of this observation we must take care not to apply it incorrectly. We cannot compare one individual with another and say that because Jones has more than Smith, therefore Jones is more in love with earthly things than Smith. Rather, we must always compare the various amounts of wealth which any individual or group might possess. Applied in this way it is always true that when a man has more the attraction is greater. We cannot compare Jones with Smith, but we can say that the more Smith owns the more of his affection and attention will be directed to earthly possessions.

A rich man will sometimes say that he is so used to handling sums of $100,000 or more that the purchase of a new $4,000 automobile means almost nothing to him. He will in this respect compare himself to some man of ordinary means whose purchase of a new car becomes a matter of idolatry. This is the kind of confusing comparison which we must refuse to entertain. We must ask the rich man, not how much the new car engages his affections, but to what extent his total financial operation has assumed the central place in his life.

"The heart of man is deceitful above all things," as the Old Testament tells us, "who can know it?" It is possible for a man even to be deceived about what is going on in his own heart. But he who knows the hearts of men has revealed the truth for us if we will but hear it. He says, "Where your treasure is, there will your heart be also."

As he continues to elaborate the same theme in Matt 6, Jesus goes on to show how serious is the subject under discussion. For one thing, he says, "If your eye is sound, your whole body will be full of life; but if your eye is not sound, your whole body will be full of darkness. If then the light in you is darkness, how great is the darkness." His subject in these words is still that of the disciple's relationship to money and possessions. He says, if you are disobedient at this point it spoils everything. To have your eye on accumulating treasures on earth just throws darkness over the whole operation.

This leads to the shocking conclusion that "you cannot serve God and Mammon." Here Jesus faces the disciple with an either/or proposition. You cannot choose both. Here is God on the one side, Mammon on the other. Whom will you serve? The word "Mammon" does not refer to evil in general, nor does it describe the Devil in all his works. Jesus is talking here specifically about money. Mammon is the god of wealth. You cannot, Jesus said, serve the God of the Christian community and the god of the financial community at the same time. So sharp is the difference in approach.

Clarence Jordan has aptly observed:

> Notice that he doesn't say that you shouldn't serve two masters, but that you can't. This isn't advice—it's law, as inexorable as the law

of gravity. It's like stating that you can't follow a road that forks. It is based on the assumption that the mind of God and the mind of the secular world are in direct contradiction to each other. They give two conflicting standards of measurement. Loyalty must be given to one or the other; it cannot be given to both. It won't work, either, to hire out to Mammon and give a tenth of your wages to God. Not even if you raise his cut to a fifth, or a half.[1]

Here are two approaches to life. Since they move in opposite directions you can't be moving both ways at once. The one approach says that the more you possess the better it is. Those who follow this rule of life therefore seek to increase their possessions. This is what they work for. They plan and strive in order to gain a bigger farm, to live in a better house, to have a larger bank account, or to drive a finer car. This is one approach.

The other approach to life is based on the insight that laying up treasure on earth is a foolish and dangerous thing which is to be avoided. These people have something better to do with their resources. In their case the program of economic accumulation has been abandoned because both their heart and their treasure are in the kingdom of God. Their investments of time and money are all directed towards the building-up of God's people.

A third and final reason undergirds the call of Jesus to abandon the world's scheme of laying up treasures; for the disciples of Christ such *accumulation is unnecessary* (vv. 25–34). This reason is apparently more important or perhaps more different to accept since Jesus spends more time elaborating it than any other. Having told his followers not to lay up treasure, Jesus now assures them that they can live adequately without it. This is a revolutionary promise, seldom understood and seldom claimed.

Among the men of this world—that is, the servants of Mammon—such accumulation is urgently necessary. For them it is a necessary principle of life. Without it, ordinary men would perish. But not so the disciples of Jesus. To them is given this promise: "Seek first the kingdom of God and his righteousness and all these things shall be yours as well."

Jesus explains that the Father knows we need food and clothing. It is not that he expects us to do without these things. But they are to come to us in a different way. To the servants of Mammon, food and clothing are provided as they anxiously accumulate and lay up in store so that they shall not be destitute. But the servant of Christ shall not be destitute in spite of the fact that he has not laid up treasures for himself, indeed,

---

1. Jordan, *Sermon*, 88.

because he has not. The Christian will have "added" unto him (as it says in KJV) precisely those things which the unbelievers "seek." This happens because the Christian is "seeking" the kingdom of God. Jesus here pledges a special economic providence for Christians who dare to obey their Lord in not laying up treasure. Believer and unbeliever alike will eat bread. But one lays up for himself and the other does not. The one provides for himself and the other is provided for by God. For too long this principle of economic life has been applied only to preachers and missionaries. Jesus intends this for every disciple.

What Jesus forbids is not working but accumulating. He does not mean that all Christians should cease productive economic labor and start handing out tracts. The witness of the New Testament makes it clear that Christians are expected to work with their hands in order to provide the necessities of life (Acts 20:34, where incidentally, it is even expected of local pastors). It is not productive economic labor that Jesus condemns but accumulating the fruits of such labor to guarantee our sustenance and well-being in the future. The Christian can work and eat and live more abundantly without such accumulation than the unbeliever can with it.

As evidence for accepting the special care of the heavenly Father, Jesus reminds his hearers of the general care this same Father exercises on behalf of his whole creation. Does not God faithfully care for all his other creatures? "Will he not do much more for you, O men of little faith?" Notice that to follow Jesus in his approach to economic matters cannot be done apart from faith. Yet how sure and how reasonable are the grounds for such faith. Consider the other alternative, Jesus says, which is to take things into your own hands. What can you do about it, even if you try? "Which one of you by being anxious can add one cubit to his span of life?" If life then is something which we as men cannot guarantee for ourselves, try as we may, why should we be so reluctant to commit our way into the care of the One who sustains all life? When we do this, then just as the birds and flowers are provided for as each function in its appointed place, so the men of faith, as they are once more restored to their proper places in the kingdom of Christ, are also adequately supplied. This confidence is not held out to all men. Jesus is not saying that the ordinary course of human events will supply our needs if we just stop worrying. He is speaking of a special process which operates within the community of faith.

This point needs to be underlined because many today reject the approach which Jesus presented because of changes that have been made in the economic system during the years that separate our day from his. It may have been reasonable, they say, to do what he suggests in a rural, family-centered economy like that of Palestine. Perhaps one could live there just by working hard and without laying up for oneself. But today, in an industrial society, many of the natural safeguards and communal provisions are gone. For us such a policy would be ridiculous.

This argument proceeds from a false starting point. What Jesus advocated was not reasonable in his day. It could be accepted only by men of faith. He was not extolling or building upon the virtues of a family-centered, rural economy. Rather, it was precisely in this context that Jesus called for a new approach. He did not imply that such an economy is sufficiently trustworthy so that one can cease laying up treasure without worrying about tomorrow. The confidence which he held out was based entirely upon seeking first the kingdom of God and finding one's place within it. Within the community of faith—there and only there—it is possible to live adequately without laying up treasure. This is possible because God has promised it and because of the special forces which operate there.

The grounds upon which this confidence stands, then, have nothing to do with a rural versus an urban economy. It is not based at all upon the trustworthiness of the economy, but upon the trustworthiness of God. Without the special circumstances which pertain to God's kingdom, such an approach would be impossible in either case. Thus, the passage of time and the evolution of society do not make it less possible to follow the way of Christ. In fact, with society evolving under the impact of the Christian gospel such evolution tends to make more and more room for the expression of faith and obedience which Jesus called for.

The disciple of Christ does not lay up treasure, then, because it is unnecessary. He can live well without it. He does not lay up treasure because it is a waste of time and energy. He has better things to do with his resources. He does not lay up many possessions because he does not want to fall in love with them. He has his heart set on one thing, and it is not wealth, nor even comfort or security.

A Major Theme

The exposition so far has been guided by Jesus's presentation of the economic issues in Matt 6. It will be well for us to note at this point that what he said in Matt 6, was not an isolated discourse on a subject which did not concern him greatly. Rather, this was a major emphasis which came up again and again in the ministry of Jesus. Comments along the same line run like a refrain through all his teaching and his parables. Jesus knew that the money question was one of the important issues of life.

Karl Barth mentions this as one of five "prominent lines" along which the call and commands of Jesus always moved.[2] He mentions it first and says, "For us Westerners at any rate, the most striking of these main lines is that on which Jesus, according to the Gospel tradition, obviously commanded many men, as the concrete form of their obedient discipleship, to renounce their general attachment to the authority, validity, and confidence of possessions, not merely inwardly but outwardly, in the venture and commitment of a definite act."

It should be noted, in the light of the kind of teaching which is usually heard in the churches today regarding money, that in all his remarks on this prominent theme Jesus was not promoting or reinforcing the Old Testament institution of tithing. He was nearly always speaking, as in Matt 6, about a person's total economic position, about a "renunciation" as Barth says, or about the grave danger that interest in money will keep men from the kingdom. This matter of not laying up treasure then, was no chance remark on the lips of Jesus, perhaps incidental to the important issues, perhaps misrepresented by the ones who remembered it, perhaps misunderstood by us today. This was a clear and continuing "main line" and the total weight of testimony is overwhelming. Jesus spoke out of his own experience, and he spoke to the experience of his followers. He knew the heart of man and he knew that possessions were one of the key issues. On one occasion, for example, when a man wanted to volunteer as a disciple, Jesus told him, in effect, that he did not know what he was asking. "Foxes have holes, and birds of the air have nests, but the Son of man has nowhere to lay his head" (Matt 8:20). In saying this Jesus not only described his own material poverty but he also indicated that those who follow him must be willing to share this poverty. The apostle Paul was therefore on solid ground when he used the example of Christ in instructing the Corinthians about their proper approach to financial things. He reminded them, "He became poor that we might be made rich" (2 Cor 8:9).

In the parable of the sower, riches fill a uniquely important place. The ground which seems to be the nearest to good productive soil is that good ground where there are no rocks but where weeds grow up to choke

2. Barth, *Church Dogmatics* 4/2, 547.

out the Word. These weeds are none other than "the cares of the world, the delight in riches and the desire for other things" (Mark 4:19). The good businessman in Luke 12, who confidently expanded his facilities to accommodate an increase in production is called a "fool." "So is he who lays up treasure for himself and is not rich towards God." Or again, among those who make excuses and who therefore fail to appear at the King's banquet, "one went to his farm and another to his business" (Matt 22:5). In the parable about Lazarus, the rich man went to hell and the poor man went to heaven (Luke 16). Notice that this parable was addressed directly to the "Pharisees, who were lovers of money" and "who scoffed" at Jesus's economic teachings, (v. 14).

On one occasion Jesus even said, "How hard it is for a rich man to enter the Kingdom of Heaven. It is easier for a camel to go through the eye of a needle than for a rich man to enter the Kingdom of God" (Matt 19, Luke 18). Jesus says in effect that it is impossible. A camel cannot go through the eye of a needle nor can a rich man enter heaven. However, Jesus goes on to say, "What is impossible with men is possible with God." In making this further observation Jesus does not take away the force of the first one. He does not tell us that rich men as rich men will enter the kingdom after all. He does not suggest that they can get through even though there is no change in the relationship between themselves and their possessions. Rather, Jesus wants us to know that the power of God is so great that it can even shatter the bonds of attraction between a rich man and his money. He is saying that in the power of God it is possible, not only for poor men, but even for rich men to forsake all that they have in order to enter the kingdom. In the Gospel of Luke, the next chapter furnishes an example of this in the person of Zacchaeus. Here is a rich man who said after encountering Jesus, "Behold, Lord, the half of my goods I give to the poor; and if I have defrauded anyone of anything, I restore it fourfold." This is the thing which is impossible with men but is possible with God. Jesus then told Zacchaeus, "Today salvation has come to this house." The rich young ruler of Luke 18, whose visit with Jesus prompted his comment about the needle's eye, is an illustration of another kind. He went away sorrowfully. He did not enter the kingdom, even though according to Jesus he lacked only this "one thing." He did not enter precisely because he would not part with his wealth. His experience makes it clear that rich men who meet every other condition but who insist on hanging on to their possessions will not enter the kingdom.

The impossible possibility of which Jesus speaks does not include the salvation of men like that. It includes men like Zacchaeus.

This is not a comprehensive list of Jesus's comments about the financial issue, but it is only a quick sampling to show that he spoke of this matter on many occasions. It was a major theme in his teaching. So crucial was this point, in fact, that he made it a universal condition for discipleship. In Luke 14, he said, "Whoever of you does not renounce all that he has cannot be my disciple."

To renounce one's possessions is therefore a necessary condition for being one of his disciples. The specific way this "break" expresses itself may vary somewhat according to circumstances. But there is no way of avoiding this point.

Questions of Application

Several major considerations have not as yet been introduced into the discussion but before proceeding further a few things should be said about the questions of practical application in the church today. What would it involve if we were to listen seriously to what the New Testament says about money?

Towards a Functional Minimum

If we begin to understand how hard it is for the rich to enter the kingdom this will move us to avoid accumulating beyond the necessary minimum. We may not be able to define the exact level of affluence from which it will be impossible for us to enter the kingdom. But if we know that such a point exists, we will not walk as close to it as possible but will keep a respectful distance. Instead of thoughtlessly or even eagerly adding to his possessions the serious Christian will exercise a considerate reserve at this point. Some kind of functional minimum will be the path which he chooses. This functional minimum varies greatly from culture to culture and from place to place. But regardless of where he lives, the Christian who understands the dangers of wealth will face the concrete alternatives that are available to him with a different sense of preferences than his unbelieving neighbor. While the neighbor wants to climb the economic ladder, the Christian will want to climb no higher than is necessary for a reasonable existence.

More specifically, the command not to lay up treasures on earth will mean one of two things:

a. It will mean at least an end to further efforts at accumulation. Some people who do not already have too many possessions (and there are many in the world) will simply learn from this to be content with what they have and forget about striving for more and more.

   The concept of "contentment" is characteristic of the New Testament approach to economic matters. "There is great gain in godliness with contentment, for we brought nothing into the world, and we cannot take anything out of the world; but if we have food and clothing, with these we shall be content. But those who desire to be rich fall into temptation, into a snare, into many senseless and hurtful desires that plunge men into ruin and destruction" (1 Tim 6:9).

   > Keep your life from the love of money, and be content with what you have; for he has said, "I will never leave you nor forsake you." (Heb 13:5)

   > Not that I complain of want; for I have learned, in whatever state I am, to be content. (Phil 4:11)

   Not laying up treasures on earth and being free from the love of money will therefore mean, in many cases, simply being content with what we have, even though it is meager. It will mean being content to operate on the financial level where we find ourselves at the moment.

b. In other cases, however, these same considerations will lead to actually decreasing the number of possessions, thus reversing the ordinary trend of accumulation. It will mean liquidating assets, selling out and giving away. This too is a recurring idea in the New Testament discussions of financial affairs. In Luke 12, Jesus says, "Fear not, little flock, for it is your Father's good pleasure to give you the Kingdom. Sell your possessions, and give alms; provide yourselves with purses that do not grow old, with a treasure in the heavens that does not fail, where no thief approaches and no moth destroys. For where your treasure is, there will your heart be also."

   In this text Jesus repeats many of the ideas found in Matt 6, such as the "treasure" and the "heart" relationship and laying up in heaven where things are secure. In Matthew, the concrete instruction growing out of these considerations is not to accumulate. Here it is to get rid of things already accumulated, to "sell." Which instruction is necessary depends upon the situation of the people being addressed. This passage in Luke is significant too because here the formula given the rich young ruler is addressed in a general way to all disciples. How often it has been suggested that the surprising instructions of Jesus to the rich young ruler are due to a very special problem which existed in his life, with the implication of course, that most people and especially ourselves, do not need such drastic counsel. But here we are shown otherwise. The idea of "selling" and "giving" is placed in a much wider context. Notice too, that the disciple's willingness to sell is preceded by the Father's good pleasure to give them the kingdom. The gift of the kingdom takes the place in their lives formerly occupied by worldly business preoccupations.

In any case, whether it is to "sell" or "to be content" the Christian way in the economic world tends to move toward a functional minimum. This would guide a Christian trying to decide how to earn his living. Suppose a young man is facing two alternatives. He could farm or be a carpenter. He could do either type of work equally well. There are no significant differences, let us say, in the income or in how these jobs affect his church fellowship and service possibilities. To be a carpenter would take several hundred dollars' worth of tools. But to be a farmer would require $30,000 to $50,000 investment in land and machinery. Recognizing the dangers of wealth, the Christian would choose the carpentry job.

A similar type of application might guide a Christian who already operates a small business in deciding whether or not to expand, should he invest the money to double the capacity of the business. While there are a number of factors bearing on any such decision, we could say from the standpoint of the principle before us at the moment, that if he could make a decent livelihood by operating the business at its present level, his extra money would be more fruitfully reinvested in missions than in increasing the size of his business.

Or consider again the question of owning a home or a car. If the Christian has the option either to rent or to own, in many instances shouldn't the Christian choose to rent his home, making the capital funds needed for ownership available for immediate use in the world and placing himself in a less committed relationship to this property? In deciding whether to make the old car do for a while or to buy a newer one, similar considerations of world need and the spiritual dangers of luxury might again become important factors in the decision. These are just illustrations. Specific applications will vary according to circumstances. But the Christian who really understands the dangers of wealth will want to limit himself to basic necessities.

Some might object at this point and suggest that we really must encourage Christians to become wealthy so that they can make large financial contributions to the work of the church. A man like R. G. LeTourneau is usually mentioned and the ideal of a very wealthy man giving a large portion of his income is sketched. However, it is very significant that the New Testament never draws this kind of ideal for us.

Instead of setting up that kind of an example, Jesus chose a poor widow who had just thrown her whole living into the offering box (Mark 12:42). There, he said to the disciples, is the example I am looking for. It is in this way that the work of the kingdom is truly advanced. In fact, Jesus made the astounding claim that the widow's two mites were of greater use in the kingdom than all the proportionate giving of the many rich people. There is nothing in this example, as is often suggested, about the motives of the two kinds of givers except what can be drawn from the fact that some gave large gifts out of their abundance and the widow gave everything she had, in spite of her poverty.

Here is the important point, however. With one dollar the poor widow can "put in more" for the kingdom than ten rich givers with their millions. The proportionate cost to the giver, and not the amount given, is what counts in the kingdom. When once this point of view is understood then the justification for diverting millions of dollars from immediate use so that some future gifts of large size may be made to the church, is completely gone. The poor widow throwing in her whole living, not the rich industrialist throwing in nine-tenths of his income, is the example which Jesus chose, whether we like it or not.

Other Mandates

While the warning against having too many possessions is one of the main things which the New Testament has to say on the subject of finances, there are other considerations which enter in as well. There are other mandates or counsels which stand alongside of this one and must be allowed to speak in any given decision.

There is, for instance, the whole emphasis on giving. And while the New Testament writers never urge that Christians should become wealthy so that they can give more, they do say that Christians should work in order to have something to give. The elders at Ephesus were told to work so that they could supply their own necessities and have something to give.

There is also the basic mandate to be productively employed, to work. The Christian is expected to be a productive member of the economy. His economic policies, whatever they are, should not lead to idleness.

Another consideration is that of freedom (as in 1 Cor 7). The Christian, in considering two alternative economic policies, should keep in mind which offers him the greatest freedom and self-determination, for he is under orders from Christ.

Each of these other mandates needs to be set alongside the one about not accumulating and together they will offer guidance in making the right choice. At first thought, it may seem like some of these are contradictory. And taken all by itself, any one of them might lead a person into a manner of life which makes the fulfillment of the other mandates impossible. If someone, for instance, would think only of the matter of freedom and self-determination they might decide that this summons the Christian to be a person of at least above average means. But while the well-to-do may move about with relative freedom, they are not the only ones who can. Thus, the Christian, considering these several mandates together, will seek out those positions and those policies in which they may all be fulfilled.

Perhaps the matter seems to be getting complicated with the introduction of several different mandates. Yet even this is not all. For besides these counsels, directed specifically to the economic life, there are other considerations which enter in as well. There are the mandates to witness and to serve and to be obedient to God's will in all things. In this connection the whole concept of the Christian's vocation must be considered.[3] All of these must be given full consideration as the Christian chooses between the several opportunities before him.

The Church as the Agent of Decision

From this it can be seen that the New Testament does not give us simple answers to all of the economic questions which we face today. An element of judgment and of Holy Spirit leading must always enter in. We cannot

---

3. See Vogt, *Christian Calling*.

find in the New Testament specific answers as to whether a Christian living in New York City should buy a house or rent an apartment. Nor does it say whether he should work for Wards, become a school teacher, run a restaurant. But it does say if he isn't careful, he will sell his soul for economic gain. And it does give us a series of penetrating insights, some general instructions, and a number of examples, all of which taken together throw light on the choices before us.

Just at this point is where the church has an important role to play. In some situations, given the biblical principles on the one hand and the concrete alternatives on the other, an individual Christian can and will make the right decision. But in many other cases, the situation becomes so complex that the various factors need to be weighed in a circle of Christian fellowship rather than by the isolated Christian. Many times, the individual is so much involved that he cannot consider the matter objectively. Or he may lack experience or be limited in his understanding of the Bible. Here is an area of life in which the church as an agency for the binding and loosing of human destiny (Matt 16, 18) needs to function. It is in the circle of fellowship, where all the various gifts of the Spirit may be employed, that the Living Christ can give his clearest answer to the specific decisions of our day.

As the situation becomes more complex the necessity of the church as an agent for valid decisions becomes more urgent. And as the years go by the economic situation certainly becomes more complex. Many aspects of economic life which in an earlier day were simply allotted to man by circumstance are now the subject of conscious choice. Before the coming of the industrial society, a man did not choose his job. He was usually born into it. Each person remained in the place where he found himself, accepting both the duties and the rewards as from God. But today, many people can choose their jobs from a wide range of possibilities. In the pre-industrial society, a man did not choose how many hours to work. He worked full time. But now there is the forty-hour week for many. Some work even less. Other jobs, especially those calling for initiative, often take much more time. How do the counsels not to accumulate and to work in order that one may give, apply in such a situation? Questions of business growth and reinvestment were often quite beyond the analysis and control of men in ages past. Also, in the more primitive societies, provision for emergencies and for old age tended to be cared for more automatically. In the face of these many new questions and options which modern society presents, the need for the church as a body for counsel and decision becomes more and more important.

A Flexible Approach

Christians who listen carefully to the New Testament witness and seek to implement the specific commands of the Living Christ will not come up with the same economic patterns all over the world. This is the obvious implication of what has already been said but it needs to be lifted out for special emphasis. There is so much difference between the economic life in poor, underdeveloped nations and in the highly developed industrial economics. It is true that the basic program of worldly men is very similar in both cases. Likewise, the serious Christians in each situation will be working with the same basic presuppositions and insights. But their conclusions and specific applications will vary. Whether or not to own a home has a different connotation among the mud huts of India than it does in the richly furnished mansions of an American suburb. Whether to be in business for oneself or to be employed by another, will mean something a little different in a situation where simple agriculture is practically the only method of livelihood as over against the highly competitive and capitalized economic community. So working against the background of varying cultural situations the serious Christian community will come up with different applications even though they may start with the same basic convictions.

Indeed, it should be noted that the New Testament itself does not attempt a precise definition of "rich" and "poor." These are comparative terms whose specific content is derived from the situation in which they are used. The significance of any economic policy may only be judged in the context of the prevailing conditions of the society in which it is placed. It is obvious that a poor American might in absolute amounts have more property than a middle-class African or Burmese. This realization does not however rob these comparative concepts of their spiritual significance, as many have tried to suggest. While in terms of absolute amounts the poor of one country may be able to spend as much as the fairly well-to-do of another country, this does not mean that the spiritual significance of these two positions is identical. This spiritual significance is derived, at least in part, from the situation in which the person lives. The New Testament, in the way it presents these issues, shows an awareness of this fact.

We might illustrate the flexibility of the Christian approach by considering how the unbelieving world applies its definition of economic responsibility. The world's principle of operations is that laying up treasure for yourself is a good thing. Riches are exalted. But this does not result in a fixed definition of wealth which is applied in all situations and to which one can aspire and then having reached it, can rest in the confidence of having arrived. Rather, this is a principle of operations that tells you what to do next regardless of where you live or where you happen to be on the economic ladder. If you are at the bottom of the ladder, this principle informs you to climb up. If in the middle-class, the instructions are still to lay up treasure. If you have just made your first million, the world's program remains unchanged. It constrains you to push on for the second million. So in the world, the program is completely flexible, completely adapted to the comparative situation in which every person lives. At any point in his economic development this worldly philosophy helps a person decide what to do next.

The Christian application of the opposite principle—do not lay up treasure—operates with the same flexibility and the same universal application. Through it the Lord does not speak only to those at one fixed place on the economic ladder. He speaks with equal relevance to the man on the bottom as to the man at the top. And what he says is not to describe a fixed pattern or level of economic life in which true happiness is to be found, rather he informs the person as to what are the next steps. He does not bring everybody immediately to the same conclusion, but he does have them all moving along the same lines.

This is illustrated in 1 Tim 6. The young church worker without significant financial holdings is told to "shun all this." He is to be content with food and clothing. However, in the same chapter there is also a word for the "rich," those who already have more than food and clothing. Notice, it is the same basic conviction which informs the action of both parties, but their action will be necessarily different because they are in differing positions. Thus, the rich are to be told, "not to be haughty, nor to set their hopes on uncertain riches but on God who richly furnishes us with everything to enjoy. They are to be good, to be rich in good deeds, liberal and generous, thus laying up for themselves a good foundation for the future, so that they may take told of the life which is life indeed."

Thus, the rich man of today may not, however, rejoice too quickly in the fact that specific counsels are addressed to "the rich." It is not as though a different principle had been brought forward for the rich. There is no permission here for the rich man to excuse his self-indulgent policies on the basis of necessity. Rather all the important notes which Jesus set out in Matt 6, are here reviewed again and applied to those who have in abundance. We hear that God supplies our every need, that those who have should give, and that in giving they lay up treasure in heaven and take hold of eternal life. Barnabas is a rich man in the Scripture who shows us what this kind of instruction looks like when it is put into practice. He not only gave of his income, but he sold a field, liquidating some of his assets to be used in meeting current expenses of the brotherhood. Thus, the application to those who have already accumulated considerable possessions gives no room for protecting self-interests. Rather it lays upon such persons an even greater burden of generosity. Just to make this clear it should be added here, that while the New Testament gives a good theological basis for what to do with wealth, it gives no theological basis for getting wealthy. Once inside the Christian church the considerations which ought to govern an individual's economic life are so different that deliberate and significant increases beyond the ordinary necessities of life should be unknown.

The flexibility of the Christian approach to economic matters, with its resultant one step at a time, is particularly fortunate in making it relevant to all, regardless of their circumstances. There is no Christian who can claim to be beyond the reach of the economic situations covered by the New Testament instructions. None, either high or low, can claim that the alternatives they face are not somehow illuminated by the New Testament witness. This also delivers us from the rigidity of trying to formulate an answer that will cover all possible cases. What matters is not whether we are doing the same thing as Christians in another state but whether we are really listening to the same Lord Jesus Christ in our own context.

Applications of the New Testament witness, then, while allowing for great flexibility will tend to move us in the direction of a functional minimum; this movement will be coordinated with the other thrusts of New Testament ethics; and the church as a functioning fellowship will be the context in which the more complicated and more important decisions will find their most valid conclusions. With these considerations in mind we can move on to continue discussing the issues of content.

Insurance

> The Lord is my shepherd, I shall not want. (Ps 23:1)

We must now say a few words about insurance. One cannot understand the Christian attitude towards insurance until he first understands the Christian attitude towards wealth. Of this we have already spoken. Like the Master whom he follows the Christian is interested in godliness with contentment, rather than in great gain.

Where this conviction is a reality the foundation upon which the entire insurance structure stands has been destroyed. The whole purpose of insurance is simply to secure for ourselves a certain level of material prosperity. It is to guarantee, by means of financial alliances, that when thieves do break in and steal and where moth and rust do corrupt, that these events will not rob us of the possessions which we have carefully collected for ourselves. Insurance is an attempt at securing the wealth which we have so that it cannot be taken from us.

For the Christian insurance is therefore unnecessary. He is not interested in laying up treasure on earth. And whatever possessions he may have at any given time, he feels no great urgency to hang on to them. Indeed, the Christian is ready at any time to surrender anything in his possession, as Jesus so clearly stated in Matt 5:40–42. Paul expressed this willingness in pointed terms when he wrote, "I have learned in whatever state I am, to be content. I know how to be abased, and I know how to abound; in any and all circumstances I have learned the secret of facing plenty and hunger, abundance and want. I can do all things in him who strengthens me" (Phil 4:11–13).

Only people who have not learned this secret need insurance. And there are many today who need it. There are many who think they know how to abound, and to be content with plenty. But they do not know how to be content with poverty and hunger (and if you look closely you will see that they are not content with their own level of abundance either). But because they have their heart set on abundance, they must have insurance. They are willing to pay sizeable sums which could be used for other fruitful purposes just to make sure that their abundance will not be taken away. For them insurance is a great necessity. But for those who have learned the secret of operating with satisfaction in either abundance or want, insurance loses its attraction. It offers something which they do not need, something which they do not desire and therefore something for which they see no reason to pay.

Some might object that insurance is not to guarantee a certain level of prosperity but only to furnish us with the necessities of life in case of emergency.

But this too is unnecessary for the Christian. For this is precisely what God himself has pledged to provide for us in any and all circumstances. We have already spoken about this in the preceding section.

As we begin to comprehend this biblical perspective on the matter, it will become clear that insurance is not only unnecessary for the Christian, but it is positively wrong. It is a betrayal of confidence, a breach of covenant in our relationship to God. God has given us his sure and certain word that those who seek first the kingdom will be furnished with something to eat and with clothes to wear, and this in spite of the fact that they do not lay up treasure. It is nothing less than faithless when one to whom God the Almighty has made this promise cannot feel secure in facing the future with only this promise but feels driven to go out and get some assurances also from Mammon—for that is who the insurance companies represent. The insurance companies base their operations entirely on the power of large accumulated amounts of money. In the United States at the present time the insurance business is second to none in the number of assets it controls. This is Mammon par excellence.

Why must the Christian make alliances and covenants with the financial powers of this world in order to obtain the same kind of assurances (though less certain and less inclusive) that he already has from the Living God? This is a betrayal just as surely as it was in the Old Testament when God's people felt compelled to make treaties with Egypt and Syria rather than to trust their defense and sustenance to God—in spite of the fact that God had time and again delivered them in ways that surpassed anything ever achieved by earthly powers.

In the book of Hebrews we read, "Keep your life free from the love of money, and be content with what you have; for he said 'I will never fail you or forsake you.' hence we can confidently say, 'The Lord is my helper; I will not be afraid. What can man do to me?'" (Heb 13:5–6)

Here we find God's economic assurances stated in the strongest and most inclusive terms. This is God's pledge. And God being God, it is beyond comparison as the grounds for confidence. It is striking to see the way the writer of this book uses two Old Testament promises. He took these promises from Deut 31:6,8 (or Josh 1:5), and Ps 118:6. In the Old Testament these promises had a rather general meaning with special reference to the matter of deliverance from enemies in times of war. But now in the New Testament situation the writer applies these promises clearly and unequivocally to the economic life of Christians. This implies, and it could be supported from other passages, that in the changed situation between the Old Testament when God's people were also a nation and the New Testament when God's people are strangers and pilgrims scattered throughout the nations, in this new situation there is a close parallel between our economic life and their political life. Just as the world of that day threatened and tempted Israel with political destruction, so the world today threatens and tempts the church with economic tragedy. And in the same way, just as God promised to deliver Israel from the hand of her enemies and did so whenever Israel had the faith to obey God, so in the New Testament God has pledged himself to sustain his people amidst economic insecurities and threats. In any case, it is nothing less than hypocrisy to say that we believe the kind of promises set forth for us in Hebrews if we at the same time have contracted with some financial power so that they will not fail or forsake us in the time of calamity.

When the well-insured man of today gets into trouble, he does not lift up his eyes, as did the Psalmist of old, asking "From whence cometh my help?" and answering, "My help comes from the Lord who made heaven and earth" (Ps 121). No, when the well-insured man gets into trouble his help cometh from Brotherhood Mutual, State Farm, or some other insurance company. In the same manner, when someone else has an accident or becomes ill, the standard question today is not, "Are you a Christian?"—a question which would seek to discover whether God and the church are pledged to meet the emergency. Instead, people usually ask, "Do you have insurance?" The person or the power to whom we turn in an emergency is the god with whom we are in covenant. Religious professions mean very little in comparison to this fact. The god who delivers us is the god who commands our allegiance. And you cannot serve God and Mammon. Your help cannot come from both sides. From whence cometh your help?

Let us illustrate this in another way. How can anyone pray with sincerity, "Give us this day our daily bread," when in the meantime they have set up a relationship with Prudential Life Insurance company that in case their supply of daily bread is cut off the insurance company will provide for it? Is this anything but hypocrisy? In whom do we place our confidence for the future? Is it God or Mammon?

Some people will say, however, that they do not take out insurance to guarantee for themselves a certain level of prosperity, nor even to furnish themselves with necessities of life in an emergency. Their only reason for insurance is to guarantee the welfare of other people. Now this sounds like a noble motive. It is the argument for survivors insurance, or automobile liability insurance and other similar policies. It is one thing, according to this point of view, to trust God to supply our own needs. But it is something quite different to subject other people to this same condition without their consent (as in an automobile accident).

Let us note however, that God has pledged never to fail or forsake his people in their economic needs. This does not only mean that he will care for them in their personal and private needs. This also means he will stand back of them in the hustle and bustle of social relationships. God's word and promise do not only apply when we are in the closet praying to him, they apply equally when we are in a car driving down the road. His promise includes both our personal needs as well as the liabilities and responsibilities which we sustain in our relationships to other people; God's economic promises therefore cover even these social emergencies. Indeed, if his promise did not cover the extreme and difficult case but only functioned for ordinary needs, then we would have to be anxious for tomorrow after all, because it is the extreme case which always upsets us. It is always these social implications of our faith which test it most severely and which are therefore its real measure. Just as in the matter of not resisting the enemy, the real test comes when the welfare of others is at stake, so here, in the realm of finances, the question of insurance versus God's promise is most difficult when we see ourselves in relationship to others.

Besides the viewpoint just mentioned, there is an even more generous approach. Some people say they are not interested in collecting anything on their policy. Their purpose in taking out insurance is to do their fair share in bearing the burdens of society. What shall we say about this? At best it is a double-minded motivation. The desire to help ourselves at the same time as we are helping others is always present in the decision to take out insurance. This is what makes it a double-minded proposition. If our sole concern were to help other people, we would hardly think of an insurance company as the best channel for doing so. Some world relief organization or some missionary enterprise would offer a more direct approach. Or if we were so sure that we had to help cover the bills turned in to an insurance company, and if this were our only concern, we could simply send them a donation. No one ever does this of course. They want a policy. They hope they never need to collect, but the policy is there, just in case. The New Testament does not offer much consolation to this kind of double mindedness.

A further objection to the use of insurance companies as a channel for helping others is that all their work is geared largely toward some future and therefore unknown events. A good share of the money is carried in large reserve funds. When we invest our money in this way, we do not know for sure that anyone will ever benefit thereby. Only if certain future conditions materialize will the money be used to help someone. Thus, every insurance policy is based on a calculation of risks. And in most cases this speculation is in the nature of fear. People insure because they fear the unfortunate circumstances which may come upon them.

However, the Christian whose one concern is to help other people, needs not and cannot be satisfied with this kind of guesswork. He need not speculate because he does not fear. He will not, because the known needs of the present are so many and so clear that setting these aside for some possible and uncertain benefit in the future would be doubtful indeed. How it is possible, for example, for the loving Christian to set the uncertain future needs of his own family ahead of the pressing immediate needs of starving millions is impossible for me to understand. When the Lord comes all the money invested in insurance will be useless both to the ones who invested it, as well as for helping anyone else. In contrast, that money which is given to the poor of today will be certain to bear its fruit both in the present and throughout eternity. Thus, without the self-protection motive, insurance companies do not seem very well adapted as instruments of Christian love.

Jesus came to set us free from the service of Mammon. In order to do this, he substituted his own guarantees about the future in the place of those which Mammon has imposed upon the bulk of mankind through threats of poverty. "Hence we can confidently say, 'The Lord is my helper, I will not be afraid; what can man do to me?'" Hence, we need "have no anxiety about anything, but in everything by prayer and supplication with thanksgiving let your requests be made known to God" (Phil 4:6).

The question of what to do in those states where automobile liability insurance is a legal requirement is worth mentioning here. The only right way to find God's answer to this question is first to eliminate all those insurances which are not required by law and to put into practice, as a brotherhood, all those other economic principles which the gospel brings to us and which the law does not forbid. And then, when we have done all that, we will be in the right position to look at this further question. Then we can ask whether we must carry our faithfulness one step further and do that which the law forbids, or whether in this case where the law requires it of us we will go along with the powers that be. Our tendency is to want to discuss this type of problematic question first of all. This offers us a convenient way to stall any action on those many areas where what is required of us by the gospel could be put into effect immediately.

One of the things we will often discover if we take this route is that God creates new alternatives along the way so that what seemed like an impossible situation from a distance actually has within it a reasonable opening for the Christian when it is viewed more closely. In any case, such legal hurdles create no particular foreboding in the hearts of those who are willing to obey God in every situation, even when man's laws are against it, and are willing to pay whatever the costs may be in personal suffering.

Voluntary Indebtedness

> You were bought with a price; do not become slaves of men. (1 Cor 7:23)

Indebtedness is one of the dynamic economic factors operating throughout the world today. By employing this device many individuals, groups, and nations are able to accelerate their economic progress to a remarkable degree. The only price that is asked of them is their commitment to continue in the struggle for economic advancement and their promise to return a portion of the rewards to those who gave them help.

This is another area of economic life in which the Christian must part ways with his unbelieving neighbors. He who truly loves his brother and his neighbor is already committed to the maximum. All that he is and has and ever will possess has already been pledged. His total life and resources have already been claimed by Another. How then dare such a person make additional commitments? To do so implies that we have at our command certain additional resources which do not stand under this claim of Christ and the church. But as a matter of fact, everything we can possibly spare over and above our living expenses (and sometimes right out from the midst of our living allowances), all of this is already in urgent demand because of our love for one another.

In 1 Cor 7, Paul writes, "You were bought with a price; do not become slaves of men." He is speaking to those who are not in slavery. He says it should be unthinkable for a Christian to voluntarily enter into this kind of human bondage because of a prior commitment to Christ. In the same passage he tells those slaves who are already slaves and who have no chance at becoming free to "never mind." By keeping the commandments of God where they are, they can fulfill their calling. Thus, involuntary slavery, and we would add, involuntary indebtedness, has a different ethical meaning than voluntary slavery and voluntary indebtedness. The one can be accepted and incorporated in the Christian life in an excellent positive manner. The other is a denial of our calling.

Indebtedness involves a pledge to produce, over and above our living expense, a certain economic surplus which we return to the one who helped us in our time of need. Most borrowing today is from banks and other financial institutions of the world. Where the relationship is to some financial power of this kind, the voluntary indebtedness is a pledge of allegiance to the agents of Mammon. The borrower agrees to produce for them a surplus and to serve them to a certain limited extent. The reason for accepting this kind of bondage, which would otherwise be quite objectionable even to the natural man, is to obtain the aid and blessing of Mammon to meet some immediate need. How can any Christian do this? If the "unequal yoke" between believer and unbeliever means anything, anywhere, it surely applies here. Here is a yoke of legal and moral bindingness. Yet it is an optional yoke. It could be avoided if we would heed the Biblical injunction to stay clear of such unequal yokes.

Besides this, in promising to have a surplus over and above bare necessities of life we are promising to attain a level of prosperity which God has not promised to us and which we have no right to claim or expect. The biblical promises about God's care for his people always speak in the most reserved terms, such as, "daily bread," or "food and clothing." When we promise to repay a loan, we promise to secure for ourselves more than daily bread and clothing. This is a commitment which can easily discredit the integrity of God and his people because it is a commitment which he has not authorized us to make.

Related to this is the Christian reserve about the future. James says, "Come now, you who say, 'today or tomorrow we will go into such and such a town and spend a year there and trade and get gain.' Whereas you do not know about tomorrow. What is your life? For you are a mist that appears for a little time and then vanishes. Instead you ought to say, 'If the Lord wills, we shall live and shall do this or that.' As it is you boast in your arrogance. All such boasting is evil. Whoever knows what is right to do and fails to do it, for him it is sin" (4:12–17).

James says it is sinfully arrogant to be so sure about the future. But men of today, even Christian men, are going a step further. Not only do they decide what they are going to do for the next year and that there will be gain in it, they sit down and calculate just how much gain it will bring. And as if that were not enough, they go out and promise to produce that much gain. In return for this arrogant promise they are given some social or economic advantage. Like Adam in the garden, who did not want to live as God's subject but preferred instead to become the master of his own destiny, so many today are willing to take the future in their own hands and give their own word as to what it shall bring to them. It is tragic almost beyond words to see many of these people laboring under the frustration of trying to fulfill these reckless promises.

This is surely also the relevant realm of application for the New Testament prohibition on swearing oaths. God did what we are not able to do. He swore an oath to Abraham. This oath, and God's reasons for giving it, help us to understand why we cannot do the same. God gave this oath to Abraham in order to show "through two unchangeable things" (himself and the oath, Heb 6), that he would accomplish all that he had said. God could make this kind of a promise because he could keep it. But here we are as those who cannot make one hair white or black, as those who do not know the future, nor what destiny will befall us. It is therefore nothing less than arrogance for us to promise other people that our prosperity shall endure at a certain level throughout a definite period of time.

This rejection of indebtedness is not simply an academic or arbitrary thing. It becomes extremely practical. Without any difficulty one could draw up a long list of cases, ranging all the way from an elderly bishop to a young theological student, whose service to the church is definitely hampered at this time because of debts. Because of the commitments they have made they are bound to devote so much energy to making money that they are not free to serve others the way Christ would want them to. Numerous congregations find their whole existence dominated by the need to pay off debts. This intrudes and distorts the rightful discharge of all their other responsibilities.

Many have thought a little indebtedness would do no harm, especially when fully protected by assets already in their possession. Surely under such circumstances they would never be in a tight corner where they would be unable to fulfill the promise which they made to the creditor. But these assets have a way of changing values so rapidly. First Tim 6 mentions "uncertainty" as a characteristic of money. Thus, when worst comes to worst, many have discovered that their assets are so diminished in value that they are left holding the bag. The assets are gone, and the debt is not as yet paid. Those who put their confidence in uncertain riches fall into many hurtful and destructive snares.

Not only are debts wrong for the reasons mentioned above, they are also unnecessary. We are told in the New Testament that if we have food and clothing, we should be content. If Christians were content with food and clothing, or had learned as Paul said, to be content in whatever state he happened to be—if Christians had learned this lesson the reason for indebtedness would be gone. Indebtedness arises out of dissatisfaction with our present resources.

Is it not ironical that in these days of great prosperity in America—the greatest ever known upon earth—that the American people are going more and more deeply in debt? Unfortunately, Christians are right in with the rest. Appetites have increased more rapidly than the economy. People are not satisfied even with this abundance. What is it then but covetousness, when those who have more buying power than any other people since the time of creation feel it necessary to enlarge this superabundance by spending or investing their money before it is earned. It is already doubtful that we have the right to consume that which we legally possess. But it is nothing other than greed and thanklessness that at this very time so many Christians should be so dissatisfied as to take matters into their own hands and get more money from Mammon, since God has not seen fit to prosper them beyond their present level. There is no necessity for incurring debts if Christians are content with food and clothing, or even, as Paul says, with hunger and poverty.

Perhaps someone will say, it is necessary for me to borrow money even for food and clothing. The biblical answer is that we should pray. When we pray, God acts. New resources enter the picture, in this case often the resources of other Christians who are in better circumstances. It is the lack of prayer (with all that this implies about faith and obedience), as well as the desire for more than we have, which gives rise to indebtedness.

Borrowing from other Christians is, of course, something quite different than borrowing from banks and loan companies, which are nothing other than agents of Mammon. Fellow Christians could accept and understand all that "if the Lord wills" contains as the necessary qualification for any future planning of the Christian. But even borrowing from another Christian is second best. If needs are expressed within the church, is not giving rather than loaning the appropriate Christian response? And if there is repayment by the one who has been helped, why should it not go to some other person in need instead of back to the original giver? The least that can be expected in the church is that such loans would be made, "expecting nothing in return" (Luke 6). And in most cases, it would be better if understood as an outright gift from the very beginning.

The fact that Jesus told his disciples to loan to anyone who tries to borrow from you, does not mean that the disciples therefore have encouragement or justification to go around borrowing money, any more than his instructions about turning the other cheek give Christian people grounds for striking someone.

It is to God and the church then, that we should turn in our time of need, instead of going to Mammon and his agents. This is a two-fold challenge. Many times today the church has no opportunity to help its members because Christians are more willing to confess their needs to a banker than to a brother. We are therefore challenged to bring our needs to the church. Again, it seems that often the financial powers of the world are more ready to lend their aid than are Christian brethren. The challenge is also to meet every real need which is presented.

To maintain the integrity of the church in relation to debts has a bearing on the integrity of the church in other realms of life. For instance, as the Christian becomes involved in loaning and borrowing the pressure grows for a compromise on non-resistance. Of this there is much contemporary evidence among the churches. This reminds us that there is a similar relationship between the church and the world in both political and economic life. The two realms are not identical, but similar. The life of unbelieving society would be impossible without the sword on the one hand, and wealth on the other. Society as a whole, governed as it is by sin, depends upon these powers to keep it functioning. The Christians who live within that society therefore benefit in certain ways because wealth and sword exist. They accept these benefits with thanksgiving, knowing that God has ordained these world powers to be the ministers "for good" in the present age (Rom 13). While accepting these benefits, the Christian declines any active part in maintaining either sword or wealth. The reasons are both positive and negative. He declines these functions because there are greater and more demanding functions which are required of him. These functions can be fulfilled only by Christians, whereas many people are qualified to perform the other functions. Christians also refuse this participation because they cannot do two completely contrary things at the same time. The Christian cannot at the same time be loving people and using the sword on them. He cannot at the same time be giving all and gathering all that is possible. This is the negative side.

The Christian's refusal to take a primary responsibility for these two functions, does not mean that he breaks off all relationships with society to live in isolation. He maintains an active place in both political and economic life. But it is the place of "strangers and pilgrims" rather than that of governors and capitalists. Not only is this contact maintained, the contribution which Christians make in the role of "strangers and pilgrims" is sufficiently real that they cannot justly be charged with being irresponsible parasites in society. If exercised in a true Christian way, their contribution is in fact, more responsible and more fruitful than that of any other segment of the population.

The rejection of voluntary indebtedness, then is one aspect of the Christian's discriminating relationship to society. This does not take the Christian out of the marketplace but gives him a unique place within it. This is the glorious freedom of the children of God. God in his grace has granted us to be free from the tyrannies of the powers of this world. We are therefore free to serve him, free to share with those in need, free to seek his blessing and help in times of our own poverty and distress. Who should want to find a better creditor than the one who offered his own Son in order to pay our debts? He made himself poor that we might become rich. Since God "did not spare His own Son, but gave him up for us all, will he not also give us all things with him?" (Rom 8).

Brotherly Sharing

> No one said that any of the things which he possessed were his own. (Acts 4:32)

Men usually take it for granted that to possess something gives one the right to consume it himself or to use it according to his own desires. That this is true not only in the world-at-large, but among many so-called Christians is obvious from the fact that even in the churches people with better incomes usually live in better homes, eat better food, drive better cars, spend more on clothing, recreation and education than do their brethren with less income even though they may belong to the same congregation. Thus, it is clear that those who possess money and property usually feel they have the right to use these things for their own benefit.

But this is not the way of Christian love. The true Christian must overcome this accepted way of life, both for himself and for his brethren. Instead, the Christian realizes that even though he may possess or control certain assets, they are not his own to use at will. This was given its classical expression in the early days of the church when, "no one said that any of the things which he possessed were his own."

This makes it clear that the crucial issue for Christians is not a particular form of common ownership but a unique form of common consumption. To have "all things in common" did not mean that no one any longer "possessed" anything. Because of circumstances and customs, the disposition of material assets will usually fall into the hands of certain specific people. There early Christians still speak about the things which various believers "possessed."

The unique thing was not that no one possessed anything, but that no one said any of the things which he did possess were his own. Thus, the spirit of love broke through the ordinary barriers of the economic order. The believers understood that even though they legally held title to certain assets this did not mean that these assets were to be disposed of at their own private discretion. Rather, they understood that this property was at the disposal of the entire brotherhood, according to need. This is the Christian concept of consumption. It does not depend so much on the re-shuffling of title deeds or the placing of all money in a single bank account (although these in some cases may be helpful), as upon the willingness of each member to put his entire resources at the disposal of the church.

This kind of holding "all things in common" did not stop at Jerusalem. It is reflected throughout the New Testament experience. However, in an eagerness to get around it today, many people give a false description to what happened at Jerusalem. And then they fail to see it anywhere else. As a matter of fact, however, this kind of *koinonia* became a mark of the Christian fellowship throughout the Empire. In Romans, for example, a letter written at a time and to a church which was quite removed from Jerusalem, the apostle instructs Christians to practice *koinonia* with respect to the needs of the saints (12:13). To practice *koinonia* means to make things common, that is to share. They are instructed here to do the very thing which was done at Jerusalem. The instruction is mentioned briefly along with other ethical points which indicates that Paul expected it to be understood and practiced without a detailed explanation or a weighty argument. These Christians were already acquainted with the fact that within the new community of God's people a new system of distribution was functioning which affected material resources just as much as spiritual gifts. Within this new "economy" every gift and every blessing, rather than being used to advance the welfare or prestige of the one to whom it is given, is put into the common service of the whole body. Each member is thus engaged in a process of giving and receiving, each in proportion to their abilities and each in proportion to their needs. This process cannot be reduced to a certain system or formula or fixed standard but always exists as a living process within those churches that are taking their Lord seriously. This did not happen automatically in the early days, as we may judge by the admonition which the apostle felt it necessary to give, but it did happen.

When Peter said, "Lo, we have left all and followed thee," Jesus answered: "Truly I say to you, there is no one who has left houses or brothers or sisters or mother, or father, or children, or lands for my sake and for the gospel, who will not receive an hundredfold new houses and brothers and sisters and mothers and children and land, with persecutions, and in the age to come eternal life" (Mark 10:28).

An illustration of how this actually worked out is afforded in 2 Cor 8–9. Here the abundance of the gentile churches provided for the needs of the Jerusalem believers. In their time of need, they did have brothers and sisters a hundredfold. The abundance of one group supplied the needs of the other. If the situation were to be reversed, Paul says, the flow of resources would also be reversed. Then reaching back into the wilderness experience when Israel gathered manna, Paul gives this formulation to the economic life of the church: "They who gathered much had nothing left over and they who gathered little had no lack" (8:15).

That this kind of "equality" (Paul's term) might be attempted on such a large scale would be unthinkable were not it operative within the more immediate circles of congregational fellowship. This as we know was the case in Jerusalem to begin with. It was encouraged in Rome. Something of this kind certainly existed in Thessalonica, as we can judge from the fact that some of the brethren there were trying to abuse the practice of love by living without working. That this kind of problem faces the welfare agencies of the state today but is almost unheard of as a problem in congregational life is a sad commentary on how little the church has engaged in this ministry of "equalization." The Epistle of 1 John places the willingness to engage in this kind of sharing as an absolute test of the genuineness of Christian experience (3:17).

We should also notice that one of the favorite prooftexts of those who want to lay up for themselves a little treasure or indulge in a little earthly security, is actually an illustration of this generous redistribution of resources which took place within the early Christian fellowship. "If any one does not provide for his own relatives, and especially for his own family, he has disowned the faith and is worse than an unbeliever" (1 Tim 5:8). This does not mean that we must take thought for tomorrow after all, or that we must lay up a little treasure on earth so that our families may be cared for. Anyone who has bothered to study 1 Tim 5 will know that the support of widows is under discussion. A godly widow who is left alone, we are told, should be supported by the church. The first recourse in fulfilling this obligation is to children and close relatives who are in the church. If there are any relatives in the church, they should be the ones to take care of the widow. Of course, if there are no relatives to handle it, the support of widows is the concern of the entire brotherhood. But it is in this context that not taking care of one's own family and relatives is as bad as disowning the faith. Thus, this text, along with many others, speaks of the necessity of sharing our present resources with others in the church who need them. It does not condone laying up treasures on earth in order to make the family future secure. In fact, it presupposes that this has not been done by the widows else they could care for themselves. Old people who have spent their lives and their fortune for the kingdom of God need have no embarrassment at being dependent upon the church for support in their last years. And the church is fully obligated to meet their needs. To fail to do so is a denial of the faith.

It is a further striking testimony to this mutual sharing that the Christian motivation for "work" in the New Testament is to have something to "give." In addition to the motive of presenting a good testimony to the world (1 Pet 2), and of receiving approval from the Lord (Col 3), this kind of brotherly sharing is lifted out as a motivation for earning money.

"Let the thief no longer steal, but rather let him labor, doing honest work with his hands, so that he may be able to give to those in need" (Eph

4:28). Today men work in order to get ahead, or to save for the future. But in the New Testament the goal of work is to enable one to share.

In the same vein, when Paul instructed the elders of the church in Ephesus that they, like he, should work with their hands, the overriding motivation was that they might "help the weak, remembering the words of the Lord Jesus, 'It is more blessed to give than to receive.'" Such work was also to minister to their own necessities (Acts 20:34). But above and beyond that, the real goal of work is to have something to share.

Only as we come to this final point about the practice of love within the brotherhood can we fully appreciate the earlier limitations which are imposed upon us as Christians. This is the positive side of the whole matter. The Christian does not accumulate, he does not insure against the future, he does not borrow and pledge, in order that brotherly love can function realistically.

Instead of accumulating and insuring he shares what he has with those who need it now. He can do this because he has been set free from the anxieties of the world and the drive to lay up treasures has been cut off. All his resources are set free for immediate use in and through the church. This makes possible that kind of Christian liberality and sharing which in turn is the normal channel that God uses to make good his promises about caring for believers.

Christian liberality is the positive alternative to laying up treasures for yourself on earth. This is what Jesus had in mind when he said, "Lay up treasures in heaven." In dealing with the rich young ruler, Jesus made it plain that in selling his goods and giving to the poor he would have treasure in heaven. It is just as simple as that. The same idea is present in Luke 12, 1 Tim 6, and in the important parable of Luke 16. Luke 16 is one of the clearest teachings of Jesus on what a Christian is to do with his money. Here he is speaking to that question much more directly than, for example, in the parable of the pounds or the talents. In these other two parables, Jesus simply uses an economic illustration to discuss a broader subject of productivity in the kingdom. He is not offering the successful investors as literal economic examples to be followed any more than his use of the army general in Luke 14 is a literal example to be followed. But in Luke 16, the question of the Christian use of money is under discussion specifically. The example set before us this time is that of a dishonest steward. When this steward found out that he was about to be fired, he went around canceling the debts owed to his master. This illegitimate activity showed great wisdom in that after he was fired these persons would be kind to him. So Jesus said, you are to use "unrighteous mammon" to "make friends" (v. 9). This is the Christian use of money. Christians, like the dishonest steward, recognize that their control of these finances will soon come to an end. Thoughts of a settled, long-term program are therefore irrelevant. The question is what to do in this brief period. The answer is an unusual "crash program." The action of the dishonest steward violates the ordinary canons of good fiscal policy. But under the circumstances it was a brilliant strategy. He made money serve a more lasting and more personal objective.

This is also the Christian approach. The urgency and brevity of the situation in which we stand is certainly no less than for the dishonest steward. To simply accept Mammon on its own terms, thinking that by working within this frame of reference we will in the long run reap some benefit, is therefore out of the question. A special approach is called for. We, like the dishonest steward, are to put money in the service of persons in a most radical way. We are to use money to "make friends." This is what it means to lay up treasure in heaven. This is how the currency of this world (which is passing away) can be translated into values that will abide forever. This, of course, means treasure vested in persons. The poor are the agents through whom this exchange can be made (Matt 25), and they are always and everywhere present.

Thus, the Christian alternative to accumulation in the world is to use whatever is necessary for his own immediate needs and to share beyond that (or even a part of that) with those who are poor and needy. He uses all he can spare to invest in the kingdom of God, knowing that earthly investments are constantly subject to fraud, theft, arid devaluation while the kingdom values abide forever. In the same way, the Christian alternative to borrowing from the world is to confess our needs before God and his people.

This is but one aspect of the work of redemption. But it is nevertheless typical of all the rest. God delivers us from the burden of our own past. This means forgiveness of sins. It also means, as much as is possible, freedom from debts. No longer do we live on the basis of our own past, but on the basis of his past—the death, resurrection and ascension of Jesus. We are thereby set free from the bonds of the flesh. We die to the world, in this case, the economic world. Similarly, God delivers us from our own human future. He secures for us, by his grace, a glorious inheritance with all the saints, a hundredfold in this life and in the age to come eternal life. Both our past and our future are made new.

By means of this procedure our present life is also transformed. This is how the powers of the kingdom begin functioning now. The man whose past and whose future are in God's hands has a new freedom in the present. He need not labor to make up for past deficiencies nor to offset future emergencies. He can live in the present. And for that reason, he can love his brethren and neighbors since love is always a present response to present needs. The life of other men does not contain this freedom to love others because they are so overtaxed in the service of their own past and their own future, plus of course the present. This means they have neither energy, nor thought, nor money, nor affection, to share with anyone else.

This will teach us furthermore how to grow in love. It will not be enough just to exhort each other that we should love more and share more. We love only because he first loved us. We love only to the extent that we have experienced his love. This applies in relationship to our sins. It also applies to our financial life. Only to the extent that we really commit our financial past and our financial future into God's loving care will we have significant resources for sharing with others in the present.

In this way we are further given to understand that the commands, "Do not lay up treasure on earth," "Do not become slaves of men," "Take no thought for the morrow," and others, are not so much demands as they are promises. This is not law, but grace; not a new burden but a new freedom.

This is why the man of Matt 13:44 who found a treasure buried in the field went and sold all his possessions with joy. Ordinarily to dispose of all your possessions is a painful and unpleasant exercise. But if it is a step in gaining something better, the transaction is made eagerly and with great joy. So it was with the man in the parable. So it is with every Christian who catches a glimpse of the surpassing worth of knowing Christ Jesus as Lord. For this person to yield his life to the economic instructions of the Master, counting everything else as loss, is not an unpleasant burden but a glorious opportunity.

Church Institutions—A Postscript

Since the church landscape today is so dominated by the existence and influence of large church-operated institutions a few words need to be said about the meaning of all this for these institutions.

Institutions and Wealth

A rather widespread conviction is present in the churches that wealthy men are essential for the continued operation of the large cooperative enterprises of the church such as missions or relief work. Would not the acceptance of the New Testament's sharp renunciation of wealth pull the props out from beneath such projects? Are we not therefore justified and even constrained, to encourage the accumulation of wealth so that the institutions may continue?

The answer, in a word, is no. It is true that such institutions have often leaned heavily upon the wealthy. In fact, many times the institutions have been guilty of extoling and encouraging wealth in a way that is quite contrary to the New Testament. Many ordinary Christians have been much confused by this policy. To the extent that this illegitimate dependence is actually integral to any given institution, to that extent taking the New Testament way might call for significant readjustments.

Roland Allen has predicted with prophetic insight that "ours may be known as an age of financial Christianity," just as we now look back on the period of the Crusades as the age of "military Christianity," without question there are many places in the church today where it is the power of money rather than the power of the Spirit which sustains the work. Where this prevails, we must be prepared to see important changes. But there are other institutions where this false relationship does not exist.

The answer is "no," however, for another reason. We must remember that the total result of this biblical teaching is not that there is less money available for church work, but that there is much more available. At the present time we have many rich people in our churches. But the giving is miserly and church programs everywhere are hard-pressed for money. In contrast to this, a certain unmarried school teacher who has neither capital, nor inheritance but who has caught the New Testament vision of not laying up treasure on earth, gives more per week to the work of the church than do the average one hundred members in many of the well-to-do but lukewarm churches. This New Testament approach does not dry up the sources of Christian giving, it opens a floodgate of liberality which is overwhelming whenever we can see it working.

Thus, there is no reason to soft-pedal the New Testament critique of wealth just to protect the church institutions. It should also be pointed out that church institutions have no more justification for maintaining large financial reserves than do individual Christians. Unfortunately, some church organizations have surpassed the ordinary members in their zeal to gather and maintain large funds.

Institutional Indebtedness

As in the case of accumulation so also in the matter of indebtedness the church institutions have often exceeded the ordinary members in their willingness to borrow from Mammon. This has been done in the name of spiritual progress and it is quite the accepted thing in many areas to borrow money from the world to do the work of God. But this is surely false.

The young missionary Hudson Taylor was certainly correct when he objected to the policy of indebtedness which was being followed by the Chinese Evangelization Society with which he was originally associated. Taylor wrote:

> To me it seemed that the teaching of God's Word was unmistakably clear: "Owe no man anything." To borrow money implied to my mind a contradiction of Scripture—a confession that God had withheld some good thing, and a determination to get for ourselves what he had not given. Could that which was wrong for one Christian be right for an association of Christians? Or could any amount of precedents make a wrong course justifiable? If the Word taught me anything, it taught me to have no connection with debt. I could not think that God was poor, that He was short of resources, or unwilling to supply any want of whatever work was really His. It seemed to me that if there were lack of funds to carry on work, then to that degree, in that special development or at that time, it could not be the work of God. To satisfy my conscience I was therefore compelled to resign my connection with the society.[4]

Whenever a church organization faces a lack of funds there are several legitimate inferences which can be drawn. One is the point mentioned by Taylor, that in this situation and at this time God does not want to see these funds spent in the manner intended. We must be prepared to consider this possibility more often than we usually do. Perhaps God wants to curtail a certain program or even to cut it off altogether. But what chance does he have if, when God and his people do not furnish us with enough resources to carry on, we take things into our own hands and team up with the world so that the program can go on?

---

4. Taylor, *Hudson Taylor's Spiritual Secret*, 81.

The other possibility when funds are lacking is to go before God and his people to present this need. If we would borrow less, we would pray more. This would be good. Also, the shortage of funds might be just the needed stimulus for challenging the churches afresh with their responsibilities for the work of God's kingdom. It is easier however to tell the bankers, many times, than to tell the churches of our need. And strange as it may seem, often they are more ready to help than are the people in the churches. But even though it may be more difficult and seem to bring less immediate results, in the long run it will be so much more effective to present the case to the churches. If this were done consistently then there would be less need to invent public relations gimmicks to get the churches interested in the work.

Those who are in the habit of borrowing from the world to carry on the church program have a difficult time imagining how the work could be conducted without this. But there are many sizeable Christian enterprises which have been built and sustained on a "no indebtedness" policy. Prairie Bible Institute in Alberta is just one example. Their large campus, with adequate facilities for at least 1,000 students, is proof that even large and continuing projects can be successfully sustained when God's people are determined to expend no more resources than God gives them. This may seem like a slower and more difficult way, but it is always on a much sounder basis both spiritually and financially.

Church-operated Insurance

Another facet of the institutional life of the church today is the existence of many church-owned and church-operated insurance companies. They are often called "mutual aid programs." But the basic method of operation in most of these organizations is identical to that which the world knows as "insurance." These organizations are usually identified and controlled by the state regulations covering insurance companies. If the position towards insurance is understood in the way set out earlier in this paper it will be immediately evident that these church-operated programs leave much to be desired.

They claim to be mutual aid organizations whose sole function is to equalize financial losses experienced among members of the brotherhood. However, if this and this alone were the purpose of the organization, it would be set up along different lines.

First, the process of obtaining membership nearly always involves a definition of the kind and the amounts of help which the new member will receive if and when he faces an emergency. Thus, it is clear that the thrust is identical to the insurance companies of the world. The emphasis is clearly upon the protection of our own future. In a genuine mutual aid program where the fear of the future has been banished, the focus of attention would be on the existent needs of others which are to be served. In this context it would be an idle waste of time to try to project in advance how to meet emergencies which do not yet exist. The focus of attention would be, not on how our property would be protected in the future, but on what we can do now to help someone else. The basis upon which an individual would determine the size of his contribution would not be related to how much help he may need in the future but on the basis of his total resources which are immediately available, "according to what a man has" (1 Cor 8:17). The act of helpfulness is itself a sufficient guarantee for the future contingencies for all those who believe Matt 6. Any need or desire to guarantee it further indicates a lack of faith and love.

Second, by creating a mutual aid organization with its own special voluntary membership within the church, we actually undermine the possibility that the church as a church might function in this realm. The church is, by definition, a mutual aid organization. Membership in the church automatically includes unlimited financial liability for all other members of the church. While this truth is not often recognized and seldom practiced, it is only pushed further aside by the creation of special organizations with optional membership for the purpose of doing the very thing which the existing organization with the existing membership is supposed to be doing. By creating such an organization, we deny the relevance of the existing church to the task of mutual aid. When we join such an additional and optional type of relationship, we imply that the act of joining the church does not already commit us to be mutually responsible.

Closely related to this is the fact that if the church as a church were functioning in mutual aid then the congregation would be the basic unit where all normal needs are taken care of. Inter-congregational aid would function primarily in those cases where the emergency was more than the local group could handle. That such routine things as paying for the birth of babies is taken care of via a national office, instead of by a local congregation, is another indication of how far the creation of special insurance companies within the church has actually undermined the functioning of true brotherly care within the congregation.

Third, in these insurance companies the people who get help are the ones who pay into the program. There are a few exceptions but not many. However, often it is the people and the congregations which need help the most desperately who are unable to sustain a contributing membership in such a program. Shall they be excluded from our aid? If so, the program has lost its Christian meaning. Jesus said if we only love those who love us, we have accomplished nothing unique. Everyone in the world does that much. And what is there more than this in most mutual aid programs of the church today? The whole concept of helping where there is no prospect of having help returned has been almost lost in many of these cases. This only shows how much these organizations exist to guarantee that we shall get help rather than to make sure that others are being helped.

Finally, it must be pointed out that in the accumulation of large financial reserves the church programs are operating on precisely the same premise as insurance companies of the world. They, like worldly insurance companies, derive their power and confidence from the strength of accumulated money. The feeling that these reserves are necessary against possible emergencies shows that a trust in the Lord has been lost. There is no confidence here that God and his people are really able to meet emergencies. If the church actually believed in mutual aid the accumulated reserve would be unnecessary. We could help others in the confidence that help would come to us when it was needed. And if this thought is countered with the objection as to what might happen if "all of us" are hit by some calamity, it only indicates that we have a worm's-eye view of who are the people of God. When the financial resources of all God's people everywhere are suddenly destroyed then we shall be entering the eternal kingdom. And when that day comes all the people who have laid up large reserves in church insurance funds will be judged foolish indeed (on the order of Luke 12), because every penny thus laid by will represent an opportunity lost forever. All this money could have been used to feed the hungry, clothe the naked and send missionaries to those who have never heard. If we really had faith in God, that is precisely what we would do with the accumulated reserves, right now.

In spite of all of these weaknesses, there are no doubt some people who put their money into church-operated insurance companies out of a sincere desire to be engaged in brotherly mutual aid. Here as elsewhere God will honor the sincere intentions of his people however inadequate and distorted their expression of it may be. But it is quite clear on the other hand, that the large majority of people involved in these church-operated programs look upon this as one more way of safeguarding their own future. For them it is just another insurance program and they mention it in the same breath as all their other policies. The sincere desire of those who really want to help their brothers would bear a greater harvest of blessings, and the double-minded motives of those who are really anxious about their own future would be more effectively exposed, if the church programs were operated on a basis which befits the brotherly purpose which they profess.

14

Marginalia

JOHN HOWARD YODER

The affluence of Western society is one of those things like the weather which everyone talks about and few do anything about. Brilliant analyses in abundance by Christian and other critics of contemporary culture make clear how sweeping a challenge to Christian faithfulness, yea how great a menace to the very substance of faith, arises from the wastefulness, the calculated stimulation of desires, and the glorification of comfort which increasingly typify industrialized societies. Yet the proposed cures are little more than pleas to try a little harder, please, and to give a bit more of your surplus to church causes, pretty please, or perhaps to tithe, as Christians follow, uneasily but progressively nonetheless, the trends set by the masters of the economy.

The major text in this number of *Concern*, arising from numerous conversations and retaining an informally conversational style of presentation, begins with the tacit assumption that even in our day the Christian who reads the Bible with a believing readiness to obey will find clear and binding counsel not only about piety and doctrine but about obedience as well. If Jesus, in a largely agrarian economy, could already speak of money as a god whose service is incompatible with that of his Father, how much more, in a society where money is the key to politics, to the good life and, to "vocational" choice, must his warning be needed!

Vogt's study may be challenged for assuming too blithely that the meaning for today of what Jesus said in another setting may be carried over simply and literally; it may be that some questions remain unanswered or that some of the illustrations chosen (e.g., church-sponsored insurance schemes) are too little known to serve as good examples. But to argue thus would be to miss the point. The first question for Vogt or for his reader is not whether the samples are well chosen but whether, if Jesus's Lordship means the unseating of Mammon, Christians have found apt ways of making this clear to their neighbors and their bankers, to their children and to the sellers of securities, above all to their brethren. What is crucial about the article is not that it takes Jesus literally but that it takes him seriously.

Contemporary Response

15

All Economy Is Atheist

Towards a Non-Competitive Hope
for the Church in the World

MELISSA FLORER-BIXLER[1]

As I write these words the world is coming to grips with the wealth inequality exacerbated by the COVID-19 global pandemic. In 2020, the wealth of billionaires, mostly white men, increased by $3.9 trillion.[2] Meanwhile, it will take a decade or longer for the majority of the world to recover from financial losses that resulted from the pandemic. Global inequality, compounded by climate catastrophe, threatens to create billions of climate refugees in failed nation-states in the coming decades. In free-market industrialized nations like the United States, the hoarding of wealth by the superrich is evaporating the middle class. While jobs are plentiful, jobs wages are stagnant. The federal minimum wage remains at $7.25,[3] a rate that has not been adjusted in over a decade. There is not a county in the United States where a family can live a sustainable life at this wage.

---

1. Melissa Florer-Bixler is the pastor of Raleigh Mennonite Church in North Carolina and a graduate of Duke University (AM Religion) and Princeton Theological Seminary (MDiv). She's the author of *Fire By Night: Finding God in the Pages of the Old Testament* and *How to Have an Enemy: Righteous Anger and the Work of Peace*. She works in the areas of transformative justice, broad-based organizing, and anti-racism.
2. Berkhout et al., "Inequality Virus," 11.
3. "Minimum Wage."

A Selectively Competitive Understanding

It is from this context that I revisit the *Concern* writings on the social threat of Communism. By the time this set of pamphlets is issued in the early 1960s, the Red Scare is past and the McCarthyism of the 1950s is fading. Stalinism is defeated and the Cuban revolution is complete, the country now firmly in the hands of Fidel Castro. It is from this position, in the cooling into the Cold War, that the *Concern* writers offer a more generous appreciation for Marxism as an economic theory. Simultaneously they critique the scope of Communist goals, its underlying atheism, and its willingness to meet the goals of Communism through violence.

But at most, their prominent critique of Marxism and Communism comes in the form of anxiety about the primacy of the church as the sole bearer of the good news of social reformation. This will become a fraught task because the writers must first acknowledge that, throughout history, the church has failed in its mission to offer this good news in a tangible form. Despite this failure, the *Concern* writers, most prominent among them John Howard Yoder, call for the creation of an alternative community that lives out the depths of the social reordering of Jesus in ways that the state could never accomplish. While the authors do not advocate for withdrawal from the world, neither does their writing "include taking responsibility for the moral structure of non-Christian society."[4] At the heart of their anxiety is a competitive understanding of the social order of Marxism and the church. This competition for relevance leads the writers to overlook their own complicity in the economic system of capitalism.

The persistent concern in these essays is to convince us that the secular state offers a promise only the church of Jesus Christ can fulfill. In his essay, Albert Gaillard contrasts Communism and Christianity through the two-kingdoms narration. Communism, he writes, is "a rational explanation of the contradictions history" and concrete action in the world that attempts to bring about a just society. Christians, by contrast, live in the reality that "Jesus Christ is the Lord of their own life and of all History."[5]

At times the historical writings push beyond a two-kingdoms theology to a critique, albeit surface-level and largely inaccurate, of the worldview espoused by Communism. For Gaillard Communism assumes "extreme optimism with regard to history" born of confidence in human

---

4. Roberts, "Refiguring Tradition," 89.
5. Gaillard, "Christians and Marxists," essay in this volume, 64.

"becoming" by which societies evolve towards desirable conditions. Instead, Christianity makes the claim that Jesus is the "decisive event in history." "In Christ," writes Gaillard, "human history is potentially summed-up; economic or social upsets can henceforth change nothing." While Gaillard asks European Christians to choose between Marxism and Christianity, he offers caution to those whose anti-Marxism causes them to ignore the haunting question behind the appeal of Marxism. He notes the Catholic Church's caution not to ignore the concerns of Communist factory workers who long for social and economic liberty. For Gaillard, Communism offers the critique, but not the answer.[6]

Yoder continues along similar lines. A Christian response to Communism is a "repentant answer" because "Christians have broken the promises the Gospel makes."[7] When the church fails to offer hope to people in economic desperation, the promises of the state will fill the gap. Once again, it is the gospel that makes a promise that Communism cannot keep.

For Yoder, then, the "answer is no answer." In the same way as Gaillard, Yoder reminds readers that Christianity cannot offer a response to the desire of the church for "security" that pronounces a definitive end to Communism. Instead, Yoder centers his audience on their Christian identity. Because of the cross, Christians do not need to be effective. Because of the resurrection, Christians affirm that new possibilities for life are always emerging. Because of the ascension, Christians place their trust in the Lordship of Jesus Christ. Because of pentecost, we know that the Spirit moves through a new kind of community.[8]

The *Concern* writers speak in one voice about their objections to the desire for the "effectiveness" of Communism, the confidence that Communists place in people, and the desire to, as Yoder writes, "fulfill history by its own efforts."[9] It is assumed that we, the reader, would understand why this is not something we would want, or that this social transformation is something which Christians should resist.

The writers of *Concern* rarely turn to a critique of the political and economic system of capitalism. Only Yoder offers up an excursus on this capitulation. He is not neutral on this matter. His preference is for "orderly democracies" taking root around the world even as he understands

---

6. Gaillard, "Christians and Marxists," essay in this volume, 63–64.
7. Yoder, "Christian Answer," essay in this volume, 80.
8. Yoder, "Christian Answer," essay in this volume, 83–84.
9. Yoder, "Marginalia," essay in this volume, 92.

that the ideals of Western democracy are largely discredited, citing Hiroshima and Little Rock.

But Yoder goes further, assigning responsibility to the church for the thriving of democracies. "Free economy," he writes, "can only survive where the osmotic effect of the evangelical witness has created respect for individual and minority rights and a grasp of morality founded upon inner resources and not mere fear of punishment."[10] Yoder's suggestion is that, for democracy to develop in a healthy way, it requires "the religious rootage of these virtues." In other words, Yoder isn't dismissing the possibility of convergence or mutual enrichment between the church and a political or economic system. Yoder is simply not open to Communism being that system. Instead, Western democracy holds within it the closest moral approximation to the social ethic of the church.

For Yoder, democracy is the foil to Communism, not an unusual trope during this period in world history. But Yoder's insistence that the church has more in common with "free economy," by which he means capitalism—that the church will strengthen and improve capitalism with the church's "emphasis on individual and minority rights"—is baffling. In the 1960s the federal government was in an active campaign to segregate neighborhoods through redlining. Black GIs returning from Vietnam were offered fewer benefits, including restricted access to Federal Housing Administration home loans. Racial capitalism's dispossession of black wealth and black futures was rampant at the time Yoder writes.

A Critical Participation

In 1961, the same year many of the *Concern* articles on the economic and political movements were written, American journalist and activist Dorothy Day published a letter in *The Catholic Worker* newspaper that also responded to the relationship between the church and Communism.[11] Day writes for Christians associated with the Catholic Worker movement who were trying to make sense of their faith in light of world history, just as *Concern* writers work to address the questions of Mennonites grappling with the history happening around them.

Both Day and the *Concern* pamphlets are published within months of the Bay of Pigs invasion, the attempt by the United States to invade Cuba and

10. Yoder, "Marginalia," essay in this volume, 92–93.
11. Day, "About Cuba."

set up a puppet government friendly to the United States. The botched effort was a disaster, one that involved multiple casualties as well as US troops being taken as prisoners of war (they were later traded back for medicine and baby food, items denied the island because of US embargo).

The *Concern* essays are troubled by the anti-religiousness of Communism and its antagonism towards the church. Day does not dispute these claims. She recognizes that the Catholic Church is persecuted in Cuba. But unlike the *Concern* writers, Day roots her argument in tangible economic struggle: "the poor, the workers, organized labor, and throughout a long series of wars, 'imperialist wars,' class wars, civil wars, race wars."[12] Day writes about an organizer who was called before Joseph McCarthy's House Committee on Un-American Activities to testify. When asked if he'd ever received help from the communist he responded, "Sure I accepted help from the Communists. Who else gave us any help?"[13] For Day, the beginning of her political praxis is the call to the solidarity with the poor. Response to that call is where the church emerges.

Unlike the *Concern* writers, Day cultivates an ecclesiology that is noncompetitive with Marxism. Communism's effectiveness is not a threat to church vitality or identity. Like the *Concern* writers, she understands Communism as a response to the failures of the church. But Day diverges from their assessment of these failures. For Day, Communism is another flawed social tool among others, another potential partner in the liberation of Jesus, a movement that is transient, conditional, but that offers concrete political tactics appropriate to the church's call to solidarity with the poor.

Day does not shy away from the tension of siding with those who persecute the Catholic Church in Cuba. And she offers an explanation. The church has largely deserted the poor for the wealth and privilege afforded by the state. Fidel Castro differentiates between this church and Jesus, the former being "Churchmen who have betrayed him."[14] For Day, the issue of the church's expulsion from Cuba is complicated by power and wealth. She recalls Castro's desire for clergy and religious to stay and teach children on the island, a desperate need. In response the diocese said they "would not teach Communism to their students and Castro in his turn taunted them with the fact that all they thought of was money and property."[15]

12. Day, "About Cuba."
13. Day, "About Cuba."
14. Day, "About Cuba."
15. Day, "About Cuba."

While Yoder gives a nod to the failures of democratic values as reasons for broad mistrust of capitalist democracies' answers to poverty, eventually seeing more virtue here than in Communism, Day draws a connection between the efforts for a just society in Cuba and the worker struggle in the United States. She discusses her visits to the west coast where she witnessed "the hierarchy silent in the face of the slavery and exploitation of the bracero and the agricultural worker." She described the jails filled with resisting workers while the church shut its doors.

On Skid Row, Day recalls watching laborers wait for work, wondering where their next meal would come from. She witnesses under-the-table child labor as families tried to survive. In El Paso she discovered pro-Catholic gangs at war with pro-Castro gangs, a fictive holy war. "They might be fighting the battle of the rich, of the American corporations," she quips.

For Day, the center of her reflection is on the disparity between the Catholic Church as an institution that thrives under capitalism and Jesus's call of mission to the poor. She voices the anxieties that underlie the *Concern* pamphlets—that the church will find itself in a place of insecurity and possible persecution under a socialist state. She responds that Castro "pleaded for peaceful co-existence, and he has said that the Church has endured under the Roman empire, under a feudal system, under monarchies, empires, republics and democracies. Why cannot she exist under a socialist state?"[16] I had the same question as I read the *Concern* pamphlets. If the church will survive as a minority kingdom among the corrupted Rom 13 power of the state apparatus, why decide for free market capitalism disguised as democracy, especially as the United States watches black and Latino workers struggle under this system? Why put our trust here, as if in this we were free from capitulation to an economic system?

One reason may be that a free market offers stability for an institutional Mennonite church that had adapted well to being the "quiet in the land" of capitalism. Perhaps an irony behind the *Concern* paper specifically dedicated to a response to Communism and socialist movements is that the writers overlooked Mennonite assimilation into and thriving from within the democracy-as-free-market that was and still is the politics of the United States.

"Atheism is an integral part of Marxism," Lenin once said, a worry that the *Concern* writers air as a warning.[17] I would suggest, with Day to

16. Day, "About Cuba."
17. Quoted in Day, "Catholic Worker Celebrates."

support me, that atheism is also an integral part of capitalism. "There is an atheistic capitalism too, and atheistic materialism which is more subtle and more deadly."[18] Philip Goodchild writes about the centralizing nature of mammon as "the value of values," inherent in the forms of exchange and credit from which we cannot extract ourselves, and by which institutions are maintained. Goodchild describes the "death of God" in worship of mammon as "the reorganization of daily life. Where the activities of daily life have been ordered by the expectation of the community or obligations to a deity, economic rationalist brings and abstract symbolization of space and time. . . . Once subjected to the abstract determinations of private property and the market, daily life can become regulated by economic rationality, which had formerly been limited by a consensus on the limitations of needs."[19] The *Concern* writings, a first entrée into the developing ideas of Mennonite men grappling with institutional forms of power, skate over the surface of what is offered in the social theory of Marxism. They largely leave behind how they already write from within an economic and political system, a system into which the church has been assimilated.

It is easier to point to the boogeyman of Stalin and Lenin, to call to mind the atheism of Communism, than it is to engage with the economic theory of Marxism and its potential alliance with the church. Instead of looking towards Marxism as a potential partner, we see fear of shaping the world in a way that would distract from the primacy of the church. One must choose, we are told, between Marxism and Jesus. We are left to wonder why the same is not true for capitalism. Day recognizes that, to be in solidarity with workers requires acknowledgement that we are already entrenched in a capitalist system. There is no getting "outside" of the system, but there is a commitment to those whom Jesus tells us are the blessed of the world. Those who are "blessed" in the beatific vision are also those who suffer most under capitalism.

I suspect that the *Concern* writers are doing the work given them to do. They are theologically engaging the political movement that is at the fore of the imaginations of much of the world in their day. But we also see that fears over the situation before them lead to a lack of engagement with the theology of economics. Our theological identity takes root within economic systems. Again, there is no outside, only a porous membrane between the social order cultivated by the church and the systems of the world

---

18. Day, "About Cuba."
19. Goodchild, *Capitalism and Religion*, 28.

around us. We cannot escape them. Instead, the work before the church is to identify how our economic participation is weighted, to recognize how we are already participants, and to utilize that interrogation as part of the ongoing work of discernment as to how our lives are good news not only for those of us in the church, but for all people.

APPENDIX

Concern Republication Volumes

The original CONCERN pamphlet series consisted of eighteen volumes that were published between 1954 and 1971. What follows in this index is a complete listing of that content as reorganized in the seven-volume series published by Wipf and Stock.

The Roots of CONCERN: *Writings on Anabaptist Renewal 1952–1957*, ed. Virgil Vogt. Eugene, OR: Wipf & Stock, 2009.

CONCERN *for Education: Essays on Christian Higher Education, 1958–1966*, ed. Virgil Vogt. Eugene, OR: Wipf & Stock, 2010.

CONCERN *for the Church in the World: Essays on Christian Responsibility, 1958–1963*, ed. Laura Schmidt Roberts. Eugene, OR: Wipf & Stock, 2022.

CONCERN *for Church Renewal: Essays on Community and Discipleship, 1958–1966*, ed. Laura Schmidt Roberts. Eugene, OR: Wipf & Stock, 2022.

CONCERN *for Church Mission and Spiritual Gifts: Essays on Faith and Culture, 1958–1968*, ed. Laura Schmidt Roberts. Eugene, OR: Wipf & Stock, 2022.

CONCERN *for Church Polity and Discipline: Essays on Pastoral Ministry and Communal Authority, 1958–1969*, ed. Laura Schmidt Roberts. Eugene, OR: Wipf & Stock, 2022.

APPENDIX: *CONCERN* REPUBLICATION VOLUMES

Concern *for Anabaptist Renewal: A Radical Reformation Reader, 1971*, ed. Virgil Vogt and Laura Schmidt Roberts. Eugene, OR: Wipf & Stock, 2022.

The Roots of Concern: *Writings on Anabaptist Renewal 1952–1957*, ed. Virgil Vogt. Eugene, OR: Wipf & Stock, 2009.

    Virgil Vogt, "Foreword"

    Paul Peachey, "The Historical Genesis of the Concern Project"

    The Original Frontispiece of Concern Volumes 1–4

Concern 1 (1954)

    Paul Peachey, "Introduction"

    Paul Peachey, "Toward an Understanding of the Decline of the West"

    John Howard Yoder, "The Anabaptist Dissent: The Logic of the Place of the Disciple in Society"

Concern 2 (1955)

    Paul Peachey, "Preface"

    John W. Miller, "The Church in the Old Testament"

    Paul Peachey, "Spirit and Form in the Church of Christ"

    David A. Shank and John Howard Yoder, "Biblicism and the Church"

    Appendix: "Close communion—On what lines?"

Concern 3 (1956)

    Paul Peachey, "Preface"

    C. Norman Kraus and John W. Miller, "Intimations of Another Way: A Progress Report"

    Hans-Joachim Wiehler, "Preaching in the Church?"

    J. Lester Brubaker and Sol Yoder, "A Concern Retreat [Concern and Camp Luz]"

    Lewis Benson, "The Call: Journal of Spiritual Reformation"

    Notes on books

APPENDIX: *CONCERN* REPUBLICATION VOLUMES

CONCERN 4 (June 1957)

  Paul Peachey, "Preface"

  "Epistolary: An Exchange by Letter"

  Paul Peachey, "What Is CONCERN?"

  John Howard Yoder, "What Are Our Concerns?"

  John W. Miller, "Organization and Church"

  Herbert Klassen, "Property: A Problem in Christian Ethics"

CONCERN *for Education: Essays on Christian Higher Education, 1958-1966*, ed. Virgil Vogt. Eugene, OR: Wipf & Stock, 2010.

  Virgil Vogt, "Editor's Note"

  Michael Cartwright, "Foreword"

  John Howard Yoder, "Christian Education: Doctrinal Orientation" (1959)

  John Howard Yoder, "A Syllabus of Issues Facing the Church College" (1964)

  John Howard Yoder and Paul M. Lederach, "Theological Statements for a Philosophy of Mennonite Education" (1971)

CONCERN 13 (1966)

  Albert J. Meyer and Walter Klaassen, "Church and Mennonite Colleges"

  Joanne Zerger Janzen, "The Bethel Experience in Retrospect"

  Walter Klaassen, "Christian Life at Conrad Grebel College"

  Henry Rempel, "The Bluffton College Christian Fellowship"

  Steve Behrends, "Christian Communal Living on the Tabor Campus"

  [Unattributed] "Tabor Christian Fellowship Association"

  Glenn M. Lehman, "The Church on Eastern Mennonite College Campus"

  Harold E. Bauman, "The Church on Campus, Present and Future: What are the Issues?"

  Virgil Vogt, "Afterword"

Appendix: *Concern* Republication Volumes

Concern *for the Church in the World: Essays on Christian Responsibility, 1958–1963*, ed. Laura Schmidt Roberts. Eugene, OR: Wipf & Stock, 2022.

Laura Schmidt Roberts, "Series Foreword"

Laura Schmidt Roberts, "Introduction"

Gordon D. Kaufman, "Nonresistance and Responsibility" (Concern 6, 1958)

Albert J. Meyer, "A Second Look at Responsibility" (Concern 6)

David Habegger, "Nonresistance and Responsibility—A Critical Analysis" (Concern 7, 1959)

John Howard Yoder, "The Otherness of the Church" (Concern 8, 1960)

Concern 10 (1961)

Jan M. Lochmann, "Christian Thought in the Age of the Cold War"

Albert Gaillard, "Christians and Marxists"

Katharina van Drimmelen, "Where Are the Firemen?"

John Howard Yoder, "The Christian Answer to Communism"

John Howard Yoder, "Marginalia"

Concern 11 (1963)

Karl Barth, "Poverty"

Andrew Murray, "The Poverty of Christ"

R. Mehl, "Money"

Virgil Vogt, "God or Mammon"

John Howard Yoder, "Marginalia"

Melissa Florer-Bixler, "All Economy Is Atheist: Towards a Non-Competitive Hope for the Church in the World"

Appendix: Concern republication volumes content list

APPENDIX: *CONCERN* REPUBLICATION VOLUMES

CONCERN *for Church Renewal: Essays on Community and Discipleship, 1958–1966*, ed. Laura Schmidt Roberts. Eugene, OR: Wipf & Stock, 2022.

- Laura Schmidt Roberts, "Series Foreword"
- Laura Schmidt Roberts, "Introduction"
- John Howard Yoder, "Marginalia" excerpt (CONCERN 8, 1960)
- John Howard Yoder, "Marginalia" excerpt (CONCERN 5, 1958)
- Hans-Ruedi Weber, "The Church in the House" (CONCERN 5)
- Quintus Leatherman, "The House Church in the New Testament" (CONCERN 5)
- Paul M. Miller, "Can the Sunday School Class Be the 'House' within which the True Church Is Experienced?" (CONCERN 5)
- Albert Steiner, "Group Dynamics in Evangelism [by Paul Miller]: A Review Article" (CONCERN 8)
- Gerald C. Studer, "Evangelism Through the Dynamics of a Christian Group" (CONCERN 5)
- Virgil Vogt, "Small Congregations" (CONCERN 5)

CONCERN 12 (1966)

- Leland Harder, "Changing Forms of the Church and Her Witness"
- John W. Miller, "The Renewal of the Church"
- John Howard Yoder, "Marginalia: A Syllabus of Issues"
- Lewis Benson, "The Order that Belongs to the Gospel" (CONCERN 7, 1959)
- Susanne Guenther Loewen, "After Yoder: Failure, Authenticity, and the Renewal of the Mennonite Church"
- César García, "A Global Communion as a Condition for the Possibility of Church Renewal"
- Appendix: CONCERN republication volumes content list

APPENDIX: *CONCERN REPUBLICATION VOLUMES*

CONCERN *for Church Mission and Spiritual Gifts: Essays on Faith and Culture, 1958–1968*, ed. Laura Schmidt Roberts. Eugene, OR: Wipf & Stock, 2022.

Laura Schmidt Roberts, "Series Foreword"

Laura Schmidt Roberts, "Introduction"

Paul Peachey, "Churchless Christianity" (CONCERN 7, 1959)

M. H. Grumm, "The Search for Guaranteed Survival" (CONCERN 8, 1960)

Edmund Perry, "The Christian Mission to the Resurgent Religions" (CONCERN 9, 1961)

John Howard Yoder, "A Light to the Nations" (CONCERN 9)

Paul Peachey, "The End of Christendom" (CONCERN 9)

CONCERN 15 (1967)

John Howard Yoder, "Marginalia"

James Fairfield, "Tongues, a Testimony"

Herb Klassen and Maureen Klassen "You Shall Receive . . . "

S. Djojodihardjo, "An Experience in My Life"

Donald R. Jacobs, "The Charismatic in East Africa"

Myron S. Augsburger, "The Charismatic Aspects of the Work of the Spirit"

Irvin B. Horst, "A Historical Estimate of the Charismatic Movement"

Gerald C. Studer, "The Charismatic Revival: A Survey of the Literature"

Werner Schmauch, "The Prophetic Office in the Church" (CONCERN 5, 1958)

CONCERN 16 (1968)

Henderson Nylrod, "Nasty Noel"

William Roberts Miller, "Pious Jingle Bells and the Coming of Christ"

Marlin Jeschke, "Getting Christ Back Out of Christmas"

John Howard Yoder, "On the Meaning of Christmas"

John Howard Yoder and Virgil Vogt, "Marginalia: The Case Against Christmas"

Hyung Jin Kim Sun, "Global Anabaptist Movement: From Cross-cultural to Multicultural to Intercultural"

Andrés Pacheco Lozano, "Mission and Margin(alization): An Ecumenically-Shaped Anabaptist/Mennonite Approach to Mission"

Appendix: CONCERN republication volumes content list

CONCERN *for Church Polity and Discipline: Essays on Pastoral Ministry and Communal Authority, 1958-1969*, ed. Laura Schmidt Roberts. Eugene, OR: Wipf & Stock, 2022.

Laura Schmidt Roberts, "Series Foreword"

Laura Schmidt Roberts, "Introduction"

Gerald C. Studer, "Second Thoughts on the Pastoral Ministry" (CONCERN 6, 1958)

[Unattributed] "Marginalia" excerpt (CONCERN 6)

A. H. A. Bakker, "Efficiency in the Church" (CONCERN 7, 1959)

Edgar Metzler, "The Need to Which We Minister" (CONCERN 7)

Lewis Benson, "The Church's One Foundation" (CONCERN 8, 1960)

Walter Klaassen, "The Preacher and Preaching" (CONCERN 9, 1961)

William Klassen, "Discipleship and Church Order: A Review and Discussion" (CONCERN 9)

Walter Klaassen, "New Presbyter Is Old Priest Write Large" (CONCERN 17, 1969)

J. Lawrence Burkholder, "Theological Education for the Believers' Church" (CONCERN 17)

Virgil Vogt, "Marginalia" excerpt (CONCERN 17)

Elmer Ediger, "*Studies in Church Discipline*: A Review Article" (CONCERN 5, 1958)

William Klassen, "Some Neglected Aspects in the Biblical View of the Church" (CONCERN 8)

Calvin Redekop, "Postulates Concerning Religious Intentional Ethnic Groups" (CONCERN 9)

Balthasar Hubmaier, "On Fraternal Admonition" (CONCERN 14, 1967)

Don Jacobs, "Walking Together in East Africa" (CONCERN 14)

Samuel Shoemaker, "Dealing with Other People's Sins" (CONCERN 14)

Kimberly Penner, "Toward Ecclesial Practices and Notions of Authority that Embody Radical Hope"

Isaac S. Villegas, "The Ecclesial Flesh of Anabaptist Visions"

Appendix: CONCERN republication volumes content list

CONCERN *for Anabaptist Renewal: A Radical Reformation Reader, 1971*, ed. Virgil Vogt and Laura Schmidt Roberts. Eugene, OR: Wipf & Stock, 2022.

Editor's Note

John Roth, "Foreword"

CONCERN 18 (1971)

Virgil Vogt, "Introduction"

John Howard Yoder, "The Recovery of the Anabaptist Vision"

Harold S. Bender, "The Mennonite Conception of the Church and Its Relation to Community Building"

Harold S. Bender, "The Anabaptist Theology of Discipleship"

William Klassen, "Anabaptist Studies"

Walter Klaassen, "Radical Reformation"

Harold S. Bender, "The Pacifism of the Sixteenth Century Anabaptists"

"Anabaptism: An Introductory Bibliography"

Appendix: CONCERN republication volumes content list

Bibliography

Adams, Ron, and Isaac Villegas. "Post-Christendom or Neo-Christendom?" *The Mennonite*, February 1, 2013. https://anabaptistworld.org/post-christendom-neo-christendom/.

Anabaptist Mennonite Biblical Seminary. "AMBS Response to Victims of John H. Yoder Abuse." https://www.ambs.edu/about/ambs-response-to-victims-of-yoder-abuse.

Banning, Willem, and Paul Bamm. *Der Kommunismus als politisch-soziale Weltreligion*. Berlin-Dahlem: Lettner, 1953.

Barth, Karl. *Church Dogmatics*. Vol. 4, Part 2. Edited by T. F. Torrence. Translated by G. F. Bromiley. Edinburgh: T. & T. Clark, 1958.

———. "Poverty." In *Against the Stream: Shorter Post-War Writings 1946–52*, 241–46. London: SCM Press, 1954.

Berkhout, Esmé, et al. "The Inequality Virus: Bringing Together a World Torn Apart by Coronavirus through a Fair, Just and Sustainable Economy." https://oxfamilibrary.openrepository.com/bitstream/handle/10546/621149/bp-the-inequality-virus-summ-250121-en.pdf.

Berry, Malinda Elizabeth. "Shalom Political Theology: A New Type of Mennonite Peace Theology for a New Era of Discipleship." *The Conrad Grebel Review* 34.1 (2016) 49–73.

Bonhoeffer, Dietrich. *Prisoner for God: Letters and Papers from Prison*. Edited by Eberhard Bethge. Translated by Reginald Fuller. New York: Macmillan, 1958.

Brunner, Emil. *The Divine Imperative*. Translated by Olive Wyon. Philadelphia: Westminster, 1947.

Cramer, David, et al. "Theology and Misconduct: The Case of John Howard Yoder." *The Christian Century*, August 20, 2014. https://www.christiancentury.org/article/2014-07/theology-and-misconduct.

Day, Dorothy. "About Cuba." *The Catholic Worker*, July–August 1961. https://www.catholicworker.org/dorothyday/articles/246.html.

———. "Catholic Worker Celebrates 3rd Birthday; A Restatement of C.W. Aims and Ideals." *The Catholic Worker*, May 1936. https://www.catholicworker.org/dorothyday/articles/300.html.

Dun, Angus, and Reinhold Niebuhr. "God Wills Both Justice and Peace." *Christianity and Crisis* 15.10 (June 13, 1955) 75–78.

Ellul, Jacques. "L'argent." *Études théologiques et religieuses* 27.4 (1952) 29–66.

Enz, Jacob J. "The Biblical Imperative for Discipleship." *Mennonite Life* 13.1 (1958) 3–5.
Goodchild, Philip. *Capitalism and Religion: The Price of Piety*. Abingdon: Routledge, 2002.
Gorky, Maxim. *Mother: A Novel*. 2nd rev. ed. Moscow: Progress, 1954.
Hershberger, Nathan. "Power, Tradition, and Renewal: The Concern Movement and the Fragmented Institutionalization of Mennonite Life." *Mennonite Quarterly Review* 87.2 (2013) 155–86.
Jordan, Clarence. *The Sermon on the Mount*. Philadelphia: Judson, 1952.
Mehl, R. "Money." In *Vocabulary of the Bible*, edited by Jean-Jacques von Allmen, translated by P. J. Allcock et al., 270–75. London: Lutterworth, 1958.
"Minimum Wage." https://www.dol.gov/agencies/whd/minimum-wage.
Niebuhr, Reinhold. *An Interpretation of Christian Ethics*. New York: Meridian, 1958.
———. "Why the Christian Church Is Not Pacifist." In *Christianity and Power Politics*, 1–31. New York: Scribner's, 1952.
Pedersen, Johannes. *Israel, Its Life and Culture, I–II*. London: Oxford University Press, 1926.
Reimer, A. James. *Toward an Anabaptist Political Theology: Law, Order, and Civil Society*. Eugene, OR: Cascade, 2014.
Roberts, Laura Schmidt. "Refiguring Tradition: Paul Ricoeur's Contribution to an Anabaptist-Mennonite Hermeneutics of Tradition." PhD diss., Graduate Theological Union, 2003.
Robinson, H. Wheeler. *Inspiration and Revelation in the Old Testament*. Oxford: Clarendon, 1946.
Sawatsky, Rodney. "Editorial." *The Conrad Grebel Review* 8.2 (1990) iii–iv.
Soto Albrecht, Elizabeth, and Darryl W. Stephens, eds. *Liberating the Politics of Jesus: Renewing Peace Theology through the Wisdom of Women*. London: T. & T. Clark, 2020.
Taylor, Howard, and Mrs. Howard Taylor. *Hudson Taylor's Spiritual Secret*. Philadelphia: China Inland Mission, 1935.
Tillich, Paul. *Systematic Theology*. Vol. 1. Chicago: University of Chicago Press, 1951.
Toews, Paul. *Mennonites in American Society, 1930–1970: Modernity and the Persistence of Religious Community*. Scottdale: Herald, 1996.
Tse-tung, Mao. "On Contradiction." In *Selected Works of Mao Tse-tung*, 1:311–48. Peking: Foreign Language Press, 1965.
Vogt, Virgil. *The Christian Calling*. Scottdale: Mennonite, 1961.
———, ed. *CONCERN for Education: Essays on Christian Higher Education, 1958–1966*. Eugene, OR: Wipf & Stock, 2010.
———, ed. *The Roots of CONCERN: Writings on Anabaptist Renewal, 1952–1957*. Eugene, OR: Wipf & Stock, 2009.
Vogt, Virgil, and Laura Schmidt Roberts, eds. *Concern for Anabaptist Renewal: A Radical Reformation Reader, 1971*. Eugene, OR: Wipf & Stock, 2022.
Waltner Goossen, Rachel. "'Defanging the Beast': Mennonite Responses to John Howard Yoder's Sexual Abuse." *Mennonite Quarterly Review* 89.1 (January 2015) 7–80.
Wright, G. Ernest. *The Biblical Doctrine of Man in Society*. London: SCM, 1956.
Yoder, John Howard. "The Anabaptist Dissent: The Logic of the Place of the Disciple in Society." *Concern* 1 (1954) 45–68.
———. "The Christian Answer to Communism." *Gospel Herald* 54.34 (1961) 757, 758, 766.

———. "Le Peuple de Dieu et le Monde selon la Bible." *Christianisme Social* (1955) 264–77.

———. "Reinhold Niebuhr and Christian Pacifism." *Mennonite Quarterly Review* 29 (1955) 101–17.

———. "The Wrath of God and the Love of God." Paper presented at "Historic Peace Churches and I.F.O.R. Conference," Beatrice Webb House, England, September 11–14, 1956.

www.ingramcontent.com/pod-product-compliance
Lightning Source LLC
Chambersburg PA
CBHW062042220426
43662CB00010B/1609